crochet love

crochet love

27 Sweet & Simple Zakka-Inspired Projects

JENNY DOH

LARK

LARK

An Imprint of Sterling Publishing
387 Park Avenue South
New York, NY 10016

ISBN 978-1-4547-0755-4

Doh, Jenny.
  Crochet love : 27 sweet & simple zakka-inspired projects / Jenny Doh. --
First [edition].
    pages cm
  ISBN 978-1-4547-0755-4 (pbk.)
  1. Crocheting--Patterns. 2. House furnishings. 3. Handicraft. I. Title.
  TT829.D64 2013
  746.43'4--dc23
                            2013002903

Distributed in Canada by Sterling Publishing
c/o Canadian Manda Group, 165 Dufferin Street
Toronto, Ontario, Canada M6K 3H6
Distributed in the United Kingdom by GMC Distribution Services
Castle Place, 166 High Street, Lewes, East Sussex, England BN7 1XU
Distributed in Australia by Capricorn Link (Australia) Pty. Ltd.
P.O. Box 704, Windsor, NSW 2756, Australia

For information about custom editions, special sales, and premium
and corporate purchases, please contact Sterling Special Sales at
800-805-5489 or specialsales@sterlingpublishing.com.

Email academic@larkbooks.com for information about desk and examination
copies. The complete policy can be found at larkcrafts.com.

Manufactured in China

2 4 6 8 10 9 7 5 3 1

larkcrafts.com

contents

Welcome 6

Basics 7

Apple Cozy Sling 20

Binder Duvet 24

Birthday Cake Bunting
+ Cupcake Picks 27

Heart Purse 30

Granny Square Belt 36

Tic Tac Toe 41

Baby's Egg Rattle 44

Bear Ears Headband 48

Pretty Paperweights 52

Camera Strap Cover
+ Lens Cap Pouch 56

Embellished Knee-Highs 60

Skinny Scalloped Scarf 63

Soap Saver + Washcloth 66

Lemonade Coasters
+ Glass Cozies 70

Four-Fish Mobile 74

Finger Puppets 78

This Little House 83

Bunting with Hearts 86

Upcycled Chair Cushion 90

Waves Doorstop 94

Freeform Embellished Skirt . . 98

Cocktail Rings 102

Upcycled Plastic Tote 106

Toddler Crowns 110

Hanging Rings 113

Missoni-Inspired Necklace . . . 118

Mason Jar Cozies 122

Resources 126

Acknowledgments
+ Dedication 128

About the Author 128

Index 128

welcome

Zakka is a Japanese term for a design sensibility that is cute yet sophisticated, playful yet profound, contemporary yet nostalgic. Zakka's multifaceted definition elevates the ordinary and mundane to imaginative levels that make people smile.

The zakka-inspired crochet projects in this book are all about the details and unexpected charm of delicate features that sometimes get missed at first glance. It's about the liveliness found in a crocheted set of bear ears and the smile a crocheted rattle brings to a sweet newborn. With a hook and some yarn, you can crochet a Mason jar cozy, embellish a favorite skirt, or even create unique finger puppets. Without a doubt, the zakka-inspired project you make will be filled with style, elegance, and a dash of fun. After all, life is short—we may as well create things that will make people smile.

With that, welcome to *Crochet Love*, where you will learn to transform yarn, thread, and nontraditional materials into 27 different projects, from trendy wearables to cozy housewares. We'll go over the basics first, and then we'll dive right in as we fall head over heels in love with crocheting—zakka style.

basics

Gather

Before you begin the delightful projects in this book, take the time to gather a basic crochet kit. You'll use the items in the kit in almost every project, so having them on hand will be useful to you as you work through the book. Specifics on sizes and types of hooks, as well as types of yarn, will be given within the individual projects. For more about the tools, read on.

Yarn and Thread

Fine cotton thread was the traditional yarn of crochet for centuries, but today we have many more options. From thicker, textured yarns to slicker embroidery flosses and trendy baker's twine, you can find any yarn or thread to suit your particular project. In this book, we'll use the following, all of which can be found at your local craft store or online:

Acrylic yarn: Made with synthetic fibers, this is the most affordable and commonly available yarn, making it a great choice for beginners who want to practice and experiment.

Cotton yarn: A basic classic for crocheters, cotton yarn is ideal for home items, such as towels and blankets because it holds its color and feels gentle to the touch.

Wool yarn: A forgiving material, wool yarn is easy to unravel and reuse. Special care needs to be given when items made of wool yarn are washed. The combination of hot water and agitation will cause certain wool yarns to shrink dramatically. (This is what makes felting possible—the process

Basic Crochet Tool Kit

- Tapestry needle
- Scissors
- Stitch markers
- Tape measure
- Clear zippered bag (for tools)
- Clear zip-top bag (for yarn and/or thread)

of deliberately using hot water and agitation to turn a larger crocheted or knitted item into a smaller, thick piece of felt.) Some people with strong animal allergies may experience a sensitivity reaction to wool yarns.

Bamboo yarn: A relatively new yarn, bamboo yarn is lightweight, flexible, and strong yet soft. It tends to drape well, making it a good choice for garments and accessories.

Hemp yarn: Also relatively new, hemp yarn is strong, versatile, and a good alternative to wool, cotton, and synthetics. Garments made with hemp yarn keep you cool in the summer and warm in the winter.

Blended yarn: Frequently more durable, a blended yarn is made by combining two or more fibers together. Blended yarns are often more affordable for the beginning crocheter.

Crochet thread: Typically made from cotton, crochet thread is more delicate to work with than yarns, which is why it's a natural choice for lace and detail work.

Perle cotton thread: A delicate embroidery thread, perle cotton is made specifically for needlework projects. Compared to crochet thread, perle cotton is not as tightly twisted and comes in a larger variety of colors.

Baker's twine: This cotton twine has become popular among crafters for gift wrapping and home décor projects. Traditional baker's twine is red and white, but with its growing popularity, companies are now manufacturing it in many different color combinations.

Upcycled materials: We'll be using plastic bags and bed sheets as our upcycled materials in this book. To prepare them for crocheting, you will cut the bags or sheets into strips, then join the strips together. The details of how to join plastic bag strips will be explained in Upcycled Plastic Tote (page 106), and details of how to join strips of bed sheets will be explained in Upcycled Chair Cushion (page 90).

Hooks

Crochet hooks are often made from steel or aluminum, though you will also see them in plastic, bamboo, or wood. For the majority of projects in this book, metal hooks are recommended. They are generally sturdier and easier to use because they push through preceding rows of stitches more smoothly. Plastic or wood hooks can break or twist through tight stitches. However, plastic hooks can be the perfect tool if you are working with fuzzy or bumpy yarns, or chunky upcycled yarn (see Upcycled Chair Cushion, page 90) as they tend to "slip" more easily between stitches of such yarns. Steel is largely used for the thinnest hooks because it remains sturdy when made into such thin instruments. Because steel hooks are so thin, they are ideal for working with thin crochet thread.

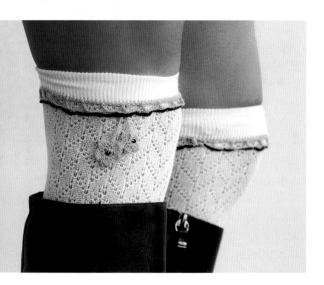

hook   throat   shaft

Crochet Hook Sizes + Equivalents (Aluminum/Plastic/Wood)

US Size	Metric Size
B-1	2.25mm
C-2	2.75mm
D-3	3.25mm
E-4	3.50mm
F-5	3.75mm
G-6	4.00mm
7	4.50mm
H-8	5.00mm
I-9	5.50mm
J-10	6.00mm
K-10½	6.50mm
L-11	8.00mm
M/N-13	9.00mm
N/P-15	10.00mm

Crochet Hook Sizes (Steel)

US Size	Metric Size
00	3.50mm
0	3.25mm
1	2.75mm
2	2.25mm
3	2.10mm
4	2.00mm
5	1.90mm
6	1.80mm
7	1.65mm
8	1.50mm
9	1.40mm
10	1.30mm
11	1.10mm
12	1.00mm
13	.85mm
14	.75mm

The three main components of a crochet hook include the shaft, the throat, and the hook. You hold the shaft, wrap the yarn or thread around the throat, and pull the yarn through a stitch with the hook. Crochet hooks come in a variety of sizes, to suit all your crochet needs. There are actually two different size systems for crochet hooks:

- **Yarn Hooks:** For these hooks, the size of the hook is measured by their diameter. As a general rule, the thicker the yarn, the bigger the hook you need. You'll see hooks labeled by both their metric size and their US size, which can be shown as a letter (B through S) or a number. The lower the number or the earlier the letter, the smaller the hook.

- **Thread Hooks:** Thread hooks are also measured by their diameter and typically made of steel. The size is indicated by a number and a metric measure; for instance, #6/1.80mm. The larger the number, the smaller the hook.

It should be noted that the various brands of hooks associate different letters with different metric measurements. For example, there is a brand that associates the letter G-6 with 4.25 mm while another brand associates G-6 with 4.00 mm. It is therefore best to look for a hook with the correct metric measurement and use the US system as a secondary reference source (see the charts at left).

There are many different styles of hooks. For example, some have an in-line throat, some have a tapered throat, some have a thumb grip, and some have ornately carved shafts. For the most part, these style differences do not affect the crochet process. Rather, they reflect the stylistic and even aesthetic preferences of the crochet artist. New crocheters are encouraged to try the many different hook styles available and discover which ones they like best.

Tapestry Needle

To finish every project in this book, you will be instructed to use a tapestry needle to weave in all loose ends. In some projects, you will use a tapestry needle to join seams together. Tapestry needles are typically made of metal and have blunt points. They come in a variety of sizes, ranging from 13 to 26. Keep in mind that the smaller the number, the larger the needle. When using a tapestry needle with yarn, a size 13 or 14 is recommended, because the large eyes on these needles will allow even thick yarns to easily go through them. For crochet thread, a size 16, 18, or 20 is recommended.

A good alternative to the tapestry needle is the yarn needle, which is made of plastic or metal. Yarn needles also have blunt points and large eyes. Both needles come with either a straight tip or a bent tip. Some crocheters like the bent tip, which they believe makes it easier to pick up stitches when joining seams or weaving in ends. Other crocheters prefer using straight-tip needles.

Scissors

Though any pair of scissors will do the job of snipping yarn for crochet, you may want to find a small, sharp pair that you can dedicate to crochet.

Stitch Markers

Especially when working in the round, crocheters often use stitch markers as a visual referencing tool, to distinguish the start and end points of a round. This helps optimize accuracy, especially when the number of stitches increases with each round.

Stitch markers for crochet are also known as split rings. They are literally little plastic rings that are split open on one side, allowing you to slip them on and off the yarn as your work progresses. Stitch markers for knitting are closed because they slide along on the needle, not the yarn. For crochet work, it is important to buy open (split ring) stitch markers rather than the closed kind. Safety pins and scraps of yarn tied into rings can also be used as stitch markers.

Tape Measure

A tape measure is a useful tool that can help measure your project. Unlike a ruler, the flexibility of a tape measure allows you to measure items that have curves and folds. A retractable tape measure is a great option for crochet because its compact size can fit nicely in your storage bag.

However, tape measures can become stretched and therefore less accurate over time. It's a good idea to use a relatively new tape measure and periodically check that it is still accurate by holding it up against a ruler or yard stick. Replace the tape measure once in a while as needed.

Clear Storage Bags

Keeping all of your tools and materials together in one place can help you stay organized. Then when you have time to work on your project, you are ready to go.

A clear zippered bag is good for keeping the items in your basic crochet kit and all of your hooks. You may find one at your local craft store, but also check the cosmetics aisle of your grocery store or drug store, which often carries several options of clear zippered pouches made of sturdy vinyl.

Rather than keeping the yarn in the same zippered pouch, use a separate plastic zip-top bag to keep the yarn for each project organized. This way, the yarn won't accidentally get tangled with small objects, such as stitch markers and tapestry needles.

Crochet Abbreviations

Abbreviations	Description
beg	beginning
ch	chain stitch
ch-(number)	refers to chain or space previously made; e.g., ch-1 space
cm	centimeter(s)
dc	double crochet
dc2tog	double crochet 2 together
g	grams
hdc	half double crochet
lp(s)	loop(s)
m	meter(s)
mm	millimeter(s)
oz	ounce
rep	repeat(s)
rnd(s)	round(s)
sc	single crochet
sc2tog	single crochet 2 together
sk	skip
sl st	slip stitch
sp(s)	space(s)
st(s)	stitch(es)
tog	together
tr	triple crochet
yd(s)	yard(s)
yo	yarn over

At its simplest, crochet instructions answer these three basic questions:

Question #1: How many stitches?

Question #2: What stitch?

Question #3: Where?

Example:

3 sc in 2nd ch from hook.

Answer #1: How many? Three.

Answer #2: What stitch? Single crochet stitches.

Answer #3: Where? In the 2nd chain from the hook.

The Crochet Abbreviations chart shown here will help answer these questions. For example, the stitch used most in this book is the single crochet, abbreviated sc. When making a project, refer back to this page if you are ever confused. It should be noted that in the world of crochet, there are many more symbols and abbreviations than listed here. Rather than listing them all, this table explains just the ones that are used in this book.

Abbreviations and Symbols

Abbreviations

Crochet pattern instructions can seem intimidating at first glance, but it's only because certain abbreviations and symbols are used that you may not be familiar with. Once you learn to recognize and work with them, the language of crochet will become second nature to you.

Symbols

Punctuation marks—the symbols in a crochet pattern—are used to give direction to the order and groupings of the stitches.

- The asterisk * symbol marks the start of a set of instructions that will be repeated, followed by the instruction "repeat from * two more times" (or the number of times to be repeated).

Gauging the Gauge

"Gauge" refers to the number of stitches and rows per inch, and it determines the dimensions of your final crochet piece. Gauge is affected by the yarn and hook you are using, as well as how tightly you are holding the yarn and hook. Gauge is particularly important to pay attention to when you're creating a garment, where the finished measurements will affect how something fits you. In this book, the projects are so small that gauge is not as significant. We provide the gauge in applicable projects, and in other instances refer you to the finished measurement of the piece.

The Craft Yarn Council's Standard Yarn Weight System chart is provided below. It outlines which type of yarn corresponds with the range of yarn weights available.

YARN WEIGHT CHART							
YARN WEIGHT SYMBOL + CATEGORIES	lace **0**	super fine **1**	fine **2**	light **3**	medium **4**	bulky **5**	super bulky **6**
TYPE OF YARNS IN CATEGORY	Fingering, 10-count crochet thread	Sock, Fingering, Baby	Sport, Baby	DK, Light, Worsted	Worsted, Afghan, Aran	Chunky, Craft, Rug	Bulky, Roving

Source: Craft Yarn Council of America's *www.yarnstandards.com*

Work the instructions between the * and the "repeat." Then go back to the asterisk and repeat the instructions.

- Parentheses ( ) are used to indicate when multiple stitches are all to be worked into the same stitch.
  Example: *(2 sc, dc) in next st*
  This line means to work 2 sc and 1 dc all into the same (next) stitch.

- Brackets [ ] are used when there are two groups of instructions nested within each other. Brackets are also frequently used for repetition.
  Example: *[sc in next st, ch 3, sk next 2 sts, dc in next st] 3 times*
  This line means you should work the instructions inside the brackets 3 times.

Getting Started

Since this is a book for beginners, we're going to start at the very beginning by teaching you how to hold the hook and yarn. We're also going to show several basic stitches, which all of the projects in this book are built upon.

Holding the Hook

There is more than one way to hold the crochet hook. The most common method is called the "pencil grip," where you hold the hook as though you are holding a pencil (1). Another way to hold the hook is called the "knife grip" where you hold the hook as though you are holding a knife (2). Whichever grip you end up using, keep in mind that you don't need to hold the hook so tightly that it becomes uncomfortable to crochet, but you do need to hold it firmly enough so that it will work for you.

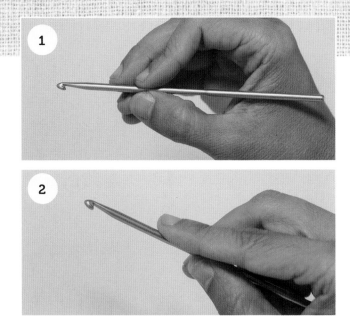

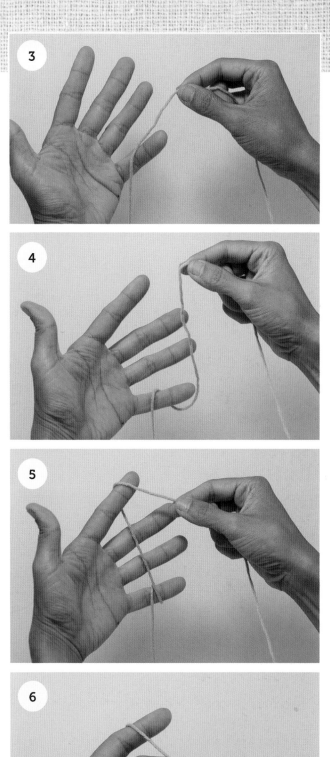

Holding the Yarn

The dominant hand holds the hook, while the non-dominant hand holds the yarn. There are many different ways to grip the yarn. The photos at right illustrate just one way:

1 With the inside of your non-dominant hand facing you, place the yarn in between the pinky and fourth finger **(3)**.

2 Wrap the yarn clockwise around the pinky **(4)**, bring it in front of the fourth and middle fingers, then place it between the index and middle fingers. Wrap the yarn counter clockwise onto the index finger. By wrapping the yarn in this way, the yarn's tension will be consistently maintained as you crochet **(5)**.

3 With the thumb and middle finger, hold the yarn and guide it while you crochet **(6)**.

Some people do not wrap the yarn around their pinky and some guide the yarn with the index finger and thumb instead of the middle finger. All methods of holding the yarn are acceptable if they are comfortable for the crocheter and get the job done.

Slipknot

Remember geometry? Remember how solutions to equations always started with "given?" This term allows problem-solvers to explain the solution without having to take the time to explain what is already known or assumed. In crochet, there is a given that beginners might not know about, because projects usually start with how many chains to stitch, like this:

To begin: *Ch 4, sc in 2nd ch from hook.*

What the pattern does not include is the step that precedes the Ch 4, which is to make a slipknot. A slipknot is something that needs to be made for almost everything that is crocheted. It is crochet's main given. Here's how you make a slipknot:

1 Fold the yarn **(7)**.

2 Twist the yarn at the fold to make a ring **(8)**.

3 Place the yarn connected to the ball through the ring to create a loop **(9)**.

4 Place the hook into the loop, and pull the tail **(10)**.

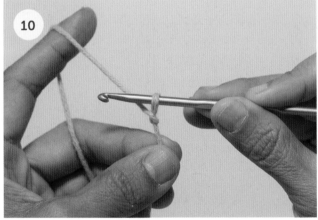

Basic Crochet Stitches

Shown here are the photos that illustrate exactly how the crochet stitches used in this book are worked.

- **Chain Stitch** (ch): Yarn over, then draw the yarn through the loop to create a new loop. Repeat to make additional chains **(11-14)**.

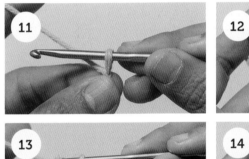 

- **Slip Stitch** (sl st): Insert hook into the work, yarn over, draw the yarn through both the work and the loop on the hook **(15 & 16)**.

- **Single Crochet** (sc): Insert hook into the work, yarn over, draw the yarn through the work, yarn over, draw the yarn through both loops on hook **(17-20)**.

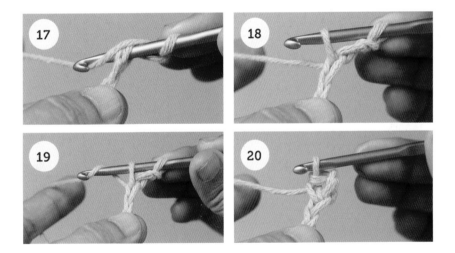

- **Double Crochet** (dc): Yarn over, insert hook into the work, yarn over, draw the yarn through the work, yarn over, draw the yarn through first two loops on hook, yarn over, draw the yarn through both loops on hook (**21-28**).

- **Half Double Crochet** (hdc): Yarn over, insert hook into the work, yarn over, draw the yarn through the work, yarn over, draw the yarn through all three loops on hook (**29-32**).

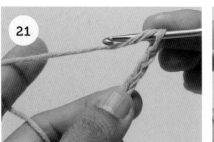

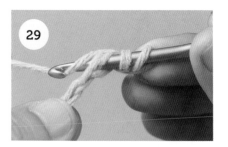

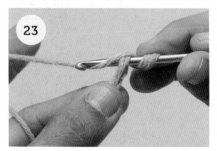

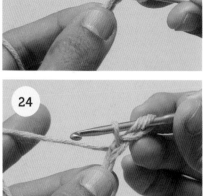

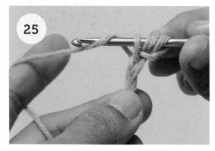

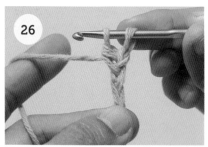

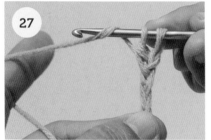

- **Single Crochet Two Together** (sc2tog): Insert hook into first stitch, yarn over, draw the yarn through the work, insert hook into next stitch, yarn over, draw the yarn through the work, yarn over, draw the yarn through all three loops on hook **(33-37)**.

- **Triple Crochet** (tr): This non-illusrated stitch is similar to the Double Crochet (dc) stitch with slight variances as bolded here: Yarn over **twice**, insert hook into the work, yarn over, draw the yarn through the work, yarn over, draw the yarn through first two loops on hook, **yarn over, draw the yarn through next two loops on hook**, yarn over, draw the yarn through both loops on hook.

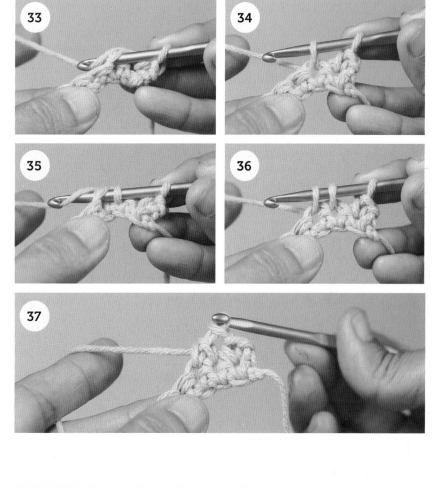

When working in rows, it's a good idea to count stitches once in a while. This can help decrease your error rate, by catching a possible skipped stitch before you've gone too far. After finishing a row, count the first stitch after the loop on the hook as 1, then count toward the other end of the row. The turning chain doesn't count unless the pattern you are following says to count it as a stitch **(38)**.

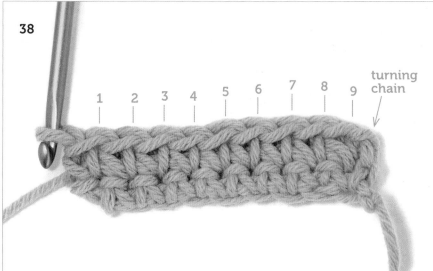

How to Crochet in a Round

Several projects in this book involve crocheting in a round. This method may feel a bit tricky at first, so the basic steps are outlined here. The first set of instructions, with figures, shows how to crochet in joined rounds to make concentric circles. The second set of instructions (opposite page) shows how to crochet in continuous rounds and allow the work to progress in spirals. All rounds (except the first round) do not end with joined slip stitches nor do they start with a ch 1.

Joined Rounds: At the start of each round, ch 1. At the end of each round, join with sl st in first sc **(39-51)**.

To begin: Ch 3; join with sl st to form a ring **(39–40)**.

Round 1: Ch 1 **(41)**, 6 sc into the ring; join with sl st in first sc **(42–46)** (you now have 6 sc).

Round 2: Ch 1, 2 sc in each sc around, join with sl st in first sc **(47–51)** (12 sc).

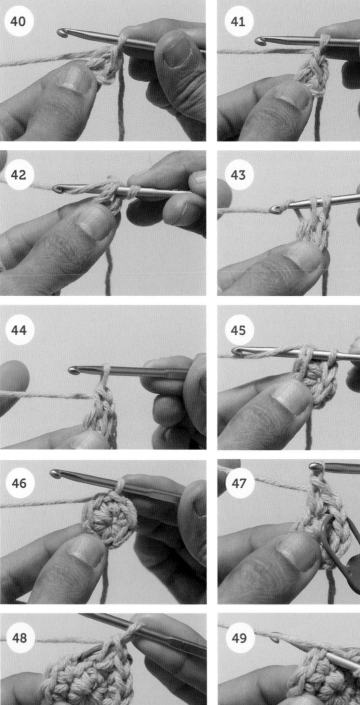

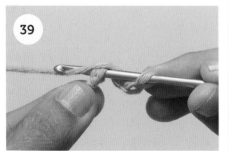

this creates a "rise" or "bump" at the beginning. So you just work the stitches until you hit the rise/bump, then you join and prepare for the next round. Having said this, some beginners still find it confusing to distinguish the rise/bump at the beginning. If this is your situation, place a stitch marker

Joining slip stitch.

at the beginning of each round, right at the ch 1, to keep things straight, and to help you learn how to notice the rise/bump.

Counting stitches after each round can also help you keep things straight. A good way to count how many stitches you have is to look at your work, and count the stitch where the last joined loop is coming out of as one stitch, then count clockwise. Another good way to count stitches in a round is to place a stitch marker anywhere in the round and then count around until you hit the marker, taking care not to count the joining slip stitch as a stitch **(52)**.

Continuous Rounds: At the start of first round, ch 1 but do not ch 1 at the start of any other rounds. At the end of each round, do not join with sl st. Instead, continue to the next round.

To begin: Ch 3; join with sl st to form a ring.

Round 1: Ch 1, 6 sc into the ring (you now have 6 sc).

Round 2: 2 sc in each sc around (12 sc).

When crocheting in joined rounds, you can see the beginning and end of the round because you have a ch 1 (or taller chains for rounds of larger stitches like hdc or dc) at the beginning of the round and

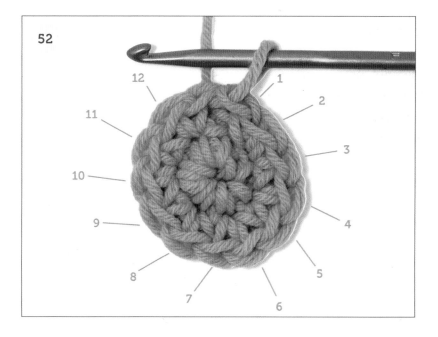

apple cozy sling

Your apple will be protected from bruising when it is nestled within this cozy. Show off your handiwork by wearing the strap over your shoulder.

Finished Measurements

- Cozy: 11 inches (27.9cm) circumference x 3 inches (7.6cm) high
- Flower: 3 inches (7.6cm) diameter

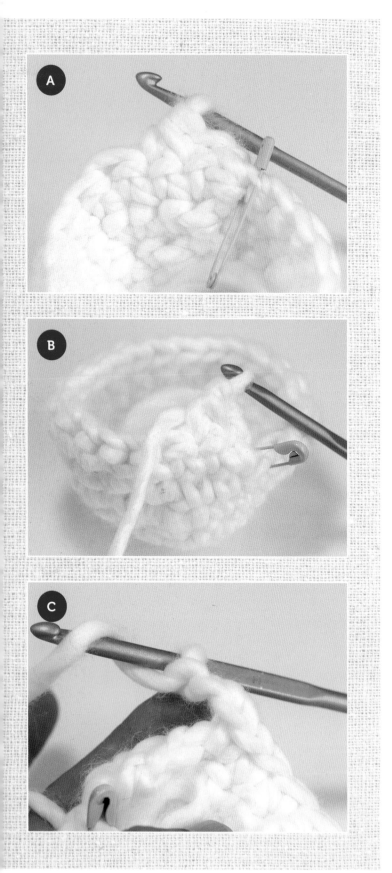

What You'll Need

- Basic Crochet Tool Kit, page 7
- Bernat Colorama (100% acrylic; 3.5oz/100g = 52yds/47m): (A) less than 1 ball, #05005 a la mode ⑥
- Loops & Threads Cozy Wool (50% acrylic/50% wool; 4.5oz/127g = 90yds/82m): (B) less than 1 ball, merlot ⑥
- Crochet hook: US H-8 (5mm)
- Large black fabric-covered button
- Hand-sewing needle and thread
- Large apple

Gauge: Approximately 8 sts and 8 rows over 4 inches (10.2cm) of single crochet

Always take time to check the gauge or the finished measurement of the project as provided.

Abbreviations: See page 11.

Instructions

Cozy

To begin: With A, ch 4, join with sl st in first ch to form a ring.

Round 1: Ch 1, 8 sc in ring, join with sl st to first sc (you now have 8 sc).

Round 2: Ch 1, 2 sc in each sc around, join with sl st to first sc (16 sc).

Round 3: Ch 1, sc in each sc around, join with sl st to first sc.

Round 4: Ch 1, (2 sc in next sc, sc in next 2 sc) 4 times, (2 sc in next sc, sc in next sc) 2 times; join with sl st to first sc (22 sc).

Round 5: Ch 1, sc in each sc around, join with sl st to first sc.

Note: Work now proceeds back and forth in rows. Do not join last stitch to first stitch in all following rows.

Row 6: Ch 1, turn, sc2tog, sc in each sc around (21 sts) **(figs. A and B)**.

Rows 7 and 8: Repeat Row 6 two times (19 sts).

Loop: Ch 18, fasten off, leaving a long tail **(fig. C)**. With tapestry needle, sew the tail to the last sc worked to create the loop for the button closure; weave in all ends **(fig. D)**.

Five-Petal Flower

Foundation Round: With B, ch 2, work 5 sc in 2nd ch from the hook, join with sl st to first sc (5 sc) **(fig. E)**.

Petals: *Ch 2, (dc, ch 2, sl st) in next sc; repeat from * 4 more times to create 5 petals.

Fasten off, leaving a long tail.

With tapestry needle, sew the flower to the top edge of the cozy, directly across from the loop. Attach a button to the center of the flower with hand-sewing needle and thread **(fig. F)**.

Fasten off.

Cord

Draw up a loop of B in sc next to button loop, ch enough sts until cord measures approximately 44 inches (112cm). Fasten off, leaving a long tail.

With tapestry needle, sew the cord at top edge, near the flower attachment.

binder duvet

Here's a great way to show off the softer side of a 3-ring binder: a duvet made of soft cotton yarns in two happy colors.

Finished Measurements

- Duvet without binder inserted, with short sides folded and whipstitched to create the flaps: 21 x 11½ inches (53.3 x 29.2cm)

What You'll Need

- Basic Crochet Tool Kit, page 7

- Loops & Threads Cotton Club (100% cotton; 3.5oz/100g = 170yds/155m): (A) 2 balls, #01444 passion pink (4)

- Lion Brand Cotton Ease (50% cotton/50% acrylic; 3.5oz/100g = 207yds/188m): (B) less than 1 ball, #194 lime (4)

- Crochet hook: US G-6 (4mm) or size needed to obtain gauge

Gauge: Approximately 2 shells over 3¼ inches (8.3cm) and 8 rows over 4 inches (10.2cm) of shell pattern.

Always take time to check the gauge or the finished measurement of the project as provided.

Abbreviations: See page 11.

Note: This binder duvet was made to fit a standard 1-inch (2.5cm) 3-ring binder. For different-sized binders, add or delete the number of shell motifs at the beginning by increasing or decreasing the number of stitches in multiples of 6.

Instructions

To begin: With A, ch 44, sc in 2nd ch from hook, *sk next 2 ch, 5 dc in next ch (shell made), sk next 2 ch, sc in next ch; repeat from * across, turn (you now have 7 full shells, 8 sc) **(fig. A)**.

Row 1: Ch 3 (counts as dc), 2 dc in first st (half shell made), * sk next 2 dc, sc in next dc, sk next 2 dc, 5 dc in next sc; repeat from * across to last shell, sk next 2 dc, sc in next dc, sk next 2 dc, 3 dc in last sc (half shell made), turn (6 shells, 2 half shells, 7 sc) **(fig. B)**.

Row 2: Ch 1, sc in first dc, * sk next 2 dc, 5 dc in next sc, sk next 2 dc, sc in next dc, repeat from * across working last sc in 3rd ch of turning ch (7 shells, 8 sc), turn.

Rows 3–18: Repeat Rows 1 and 2 eight more times. Fasten off.

Row 19: Draw up a loop of B in first st, and repeat Row 1. Fasten off.

Rows 20 and 21: Draw up a loop of A in first st, and repeat Row 2, then Row 1. Fasten off.

Row 22: Draw up a loop of B in first st, and repeat Row 2. Fasten off.

Rows 23–54: Draw up a loop of A in first st and rpeat Rows 1 and Row 2, sixteen more times. Fasten off.

The piece should measure about 11½ x 26½ inches (29.2 x 67.3cm).

Fold one of the short ends up by 3 inches (7.6cm) and whipstitch the sides together to create the first flap for one side of the binder cover **(fig. C)**. Repeat for the second side. With a tapestry needle, weave in all ends.

birthday cake bunting + cupcake picks

For an unforgettable birthday, indulge in a cake topped with a beautifully scalloped cake bunting. After the party, send the guests home with a cupcake topped with a crocheted keepsake pick.

Finished Measurements

- Bunting: 10 x ½ inches (25.4 x 1.3cm)
- Cupcake pick: 1 x ⅝ inches (2.5 x 1.6cm)

Note: Bunting can be worked to any desired length to fit the cake.

What You'll Need

- Basic Crochet Tool Kit, page 7
- Aunt Lydia's Bamboo Crochet Thread (100% viscose from bamboo; size 10; 300 yds/274m): (A) less than 1 ball #0705 pure pink; (B) less than 1 ball #0320 mushroom
- Crochet hook: US B-1 (2.25mm)
- 2 Bamboo skewers
- 2 Pieces of ½-inch-wide (1.3 cm) light blue ribbon, 6 inches (15.2 cm) each
- 2 Pieces of light blue 6-strand embroidery floss, 12 inches (30.5 cm) each
- 2 Toothpicks
- 2 Pieces of light blue 6-strand embroidery floss, 6 inches (15.2 cm) each

Gauge:

Cupcake picks: Use finished measurements of cupcake pick flag for gauge. Cake bunting: Use finished measurements of bunting for gauge.

Always take time to check the gauge or the finished measurement of the project as provided.

Abbreviations: See page 11.

Instructions

Cake Bunting

To begin: With one strand each of A and B held together, ch 3.

Scallops: *3 dc in 3rd ch from hook (scallop made), ch 3; repeat from * until you have approximately 20 scallops, or to desired length to fit your cake **(figs. A and B)**.

Fasten off, leaving a long tail.

Attach the ends of the bunting to bamboo skewers, tie ribbons and 12-inch (30.5cm) embroidery floss to each bamboo skewer, and place on top of cake.

Cupcake Picks

To begin: With one strand each of A and B held together, ch 6.

Row 1: Sc in 2nd ch from hook and in each ch across, turn (you now have 5 sc).

Row 2: Ch 1, sc2tog, sc in next sc, sc2tog, turn (3 sc).

Row 3: Ch 1, sc in each sc across, turn.

Row 4: Ch 1, sc2tog, sc in next sc, turn (2 sc).

Row 5: Ch 1, sc2tog (1 sc) **(fig. C)**.

Fasten off.

With tapestry needle, weave in all ends.

Insert toothpick through the stitches of the first row. Tie 6-inch (15.2cm) embroidery floss into bows on each toothpick.

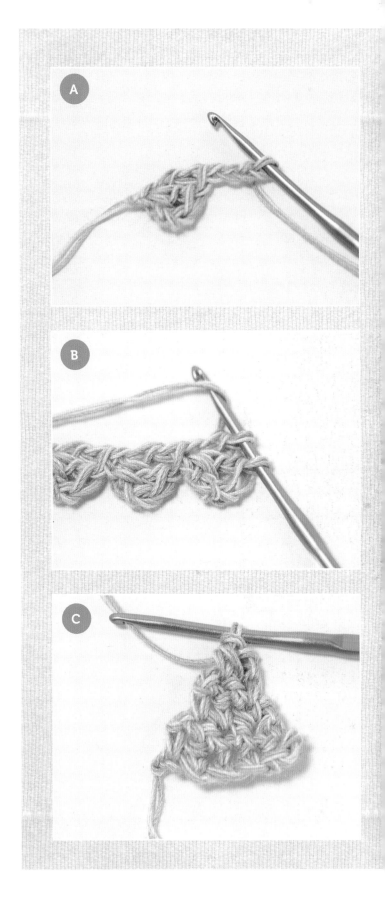

heart purse

This adorable purse is just the right size to hold your essentials: lipstick, cell phone, some change, and a credit card. What more do you need for an afternoon outing?

Finished Measurements

- Heart: 6 x 7 inches (15.2 x 17.8cm)
- Cord: 40 inches (101.6cm) long
- Picot flower: 4 inches (10.2cm) in diameter

What You'll Need

- Basic Crochet Tool Kit, page 7
- Loops & Threads Cozy Wool (50% acrylic/40% wool; 4.5oz/127g = 90yds/82m): (A) less than 1 ball, golden rod; (B) less than 1 ball, granite **(6)**
- Crochet hook: US J-10 (6mm)

Gauge: Use finished measurements for gauge.

Always take time to check the gauge or the finished measurement of the project as provided.

Abbreviations: See page 11.

Instructions

Heart: Lower Section

Note: You will be starting below the shaped tops and crocheting to the point at the bottom of the purse.

To begin: With A, ch 16.

Row 1: Sc in 2nd ch from hook and in each ch across, turn (you now have 15 sc).

Row 2: Ch 1, sc2tog, sc in each sc across, turn (14 sc) **(fig. A)**.

Row 3: Ch 1, sc2tog, sc in each sc across, turn (13 sc).

Rows 4–14: Ch 1, sc2tog, sc in each sc across, turn (2 sc).

Row 15: Ch 1, sc2tog (1 sc) **(fig. B)**.

Fasten off.

Heart: Upper Section

Hold lower section with foundation ch at top. Loosen the original slip knot, insert the hook into the loosened knot **(fig. C)**, draw up a loop of A, sc in base of next 8 ch, turn (you now have 8 sc). Place a stitch marker in the side of the last sc made **(fig. D)**.

Row 1: Ch 1, sc2tog, sc in next 6 sc, turn (7 sc) **(fig. E)**.

Row 2: Ch 1, sc2tog, sc in next 5 sc, turn (6 sc).

Row 3: Ch 1, sc2tog, sc in next 4 sc, turn (5 sc).

Row 4: Ch 1, sc2tog, sc in next 3 sc, turn (4 sc).

Row 5: Ch 1, sc2tog, sc in next 2 sc, turn (3 sc).

Row 6: Ch 1, sc2tog, sc in next 1 sc (2 sc) **(fig. F)**.

Fasten off.

Draw up a loop of A in base of same ch as the marked sc (remove the stitch marker), ch 1, sc in same st, sc in base of next 7 ch, turn (you now have 8 sc) **(fig. G)**.

Repeat rows 1–6 as above.

Fasten off.

Repeat instructions for the lower and upper sections to create a second heart.

Join the Hearts

Place the two hearts with wrong sides together. With A and a tapestry needle, whipstitch the hearts together, from one top edge all the way to the other top edge **(fig H)**. Weave in the ends.

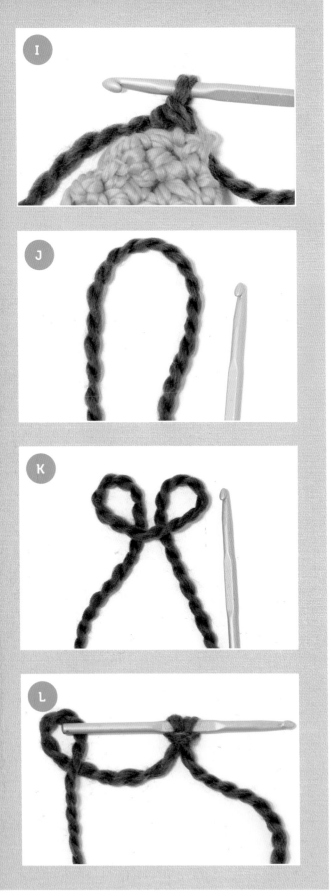

Cord

Place the hook in the top center of one upper section, and draw up a loop of B (first leg). Working away from the opening, insert hook in next st and draw up a loop (second leg/2 loops on hook), yarn over and draw through both loops on hook **(fig. I)**.

Row 1: Ch 1, turn, sl st in front loop of first loop drawn up (first leg).

Row 2: Ch 1, turn, sl st in front loop of last sl st made.

Repeat Row 2 until cord measures approximately 40 inches (101.6cm). Weave in ends with a tapestry needle.

Crochet Tatted Picot Flower

1 Cut a length of B that measures approximately 90 inches (228.6cm) long.

2 Fold one end of the yarn and place it on a work surface, with the tail on the right side **(fig. J)**.

3 Bend the fold toward you and lay it onto the work surface to make a loop that faces to the right and a loop that faces to the left, as shown **(fig. K)**. These two loops will equal one double loop.

4 Insert the handle of the crochet hook into the two loops, from right to left. Slide the double loop toward the throat of the hook.

5 Hold the yarn about 2 to 3 inches (5.1 to 7.6cm) from the first double loop and twist the yarn (as shown) to create a loop on the hook **(fig. L)**. Twist the yarn again in the opposite direction to create another loop. These two half loops equal the second double loop.

6   Slide this double loop toward the throat to create the first picot **(fig. M)**. (The picot is the loop between two double stitches.)

7   Repeat steps 5 and 6 enough times to create 10 picots.

8   Wrap the tail around the neck of the hook from front to back, place a finger between the tail and the hook to create a loop **(fig. N)**, and pull the tail through all of the double loops one at a time, using your fingers **(fig. O)**.

9   Draw the tail through the loop created in step 8, and pull to tighten **(fig. P)**.

10 Attach the picot flower to the purse by stitching the tails of the flower to the front of the heart purse, using a tapestry needle. Weave in all ends.

granny square belt

This belt shows that it's not only hip to be square, but also hip to be a granny square! Depending on how long or how short you want your belt to be, work up the number of squares that is right for you.

Finished Measurements

- Belt: 41 x 2 inches (104.1 x 5.1cm)
- One granny square: 2 inches (5.1cm) square

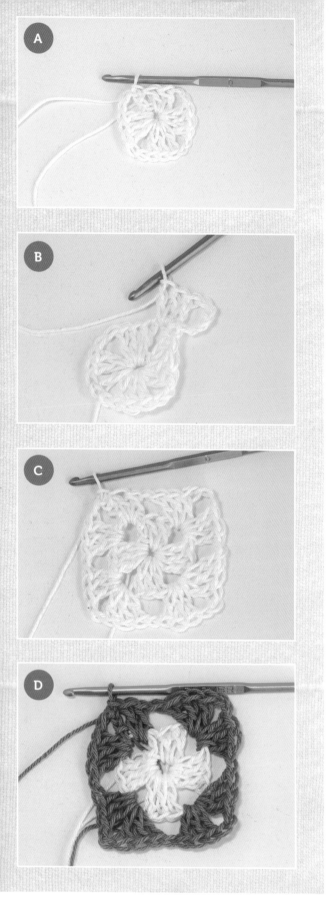

What You'll Need

- Basic Crochet Tool Kit, page 7
- Patons Grace Mercerized Cotton (100% mercerized cotton; 1.75oz/50g = 136yds/125m): less than 1 ball each, (A) #62005 snow, (B) #62436 wild berry, (C) #62044 clay (3)
- Crochet hook: US D-3 (3.25mm)
- 2 D-rings: 1½ inches (3.8cm)

Gauge: One granny square measures about 2 inches (5.1cm) square.

Always take time to check the gauge or the finished measurement of the project as provided.

Abbreviations: See page 11

Note: To make the belt shorter or longer, adjust the number of granny squares that you make and attach together.

Instructions

Single-Color Granny Square (make 8)

To begin: With A, ch 4; join with sl st in first ch to form a ring.

Round 1 (right side): Ch 5 (counts as dc, ch 2), 3 dc in ring, (ch 2, 3 dc in ring) 2 times, ch 2, 2 dc in ring; join with sl st in 3rd ch of beginning ch (12 dc, and 4 ch-2 sps) **(fig. A)**.

Round 2: (Sl st, ch 5, 3 dc) in first ch-2 sp of Round 1 **(fig. B)**, [ch 1, (3 dc, ch 2, 3 dc) in next ch-2 sp] 3 times, ch 1, 2 dc in first ch-2 sp; join with sl st in 3rd ch of beginning ch (24 dc, 4 ch-2 sps, and 4 ch-1 sps) **(fig. C)**.

Fasten off. With tapestry needle, weave in all ends.

Double-Color Granny Square (make 9)

To begin: With A, ch 4; join with sl st in first ch to form a ring.

Round 1 (right side): Ch 5 (counts as dc, ch 2), 3 dc in ring, (ch 2, 3 dc in ring) 2 times, ch 2, 2 dc in ring; to join, drop A, insert hook in 3rd ch of beginning ch, yarn over with B and draw through all loops on hook (12 dc, and 4 ch-2 sps). Fasten off A.

Round 2: With B, (sl st, ch 5, 3 dc) in first ch-2 sp, [ch 1, (3 dc, ch 2, 3 dc) in next ch-2 sp] 3 times, ch 1, 2 dc in first ch-2 sp; join with sl st in 3rd ch of beginning ch (24 dc, 4 ch-2 sps, and 4 ch-1 sps) **(fig. D)**.

Fasten off. With tapestry needle, weave in all ends.

Flower

To begin: With A, ch 5; join with sl st in first ch to form a ring.

Round 1 (right side): Ch 1, 10 sc in ring; join with sl st in first sc (10 sc).

Round 2: Ch 1, 2 sc in each sc around; join with sl st in first sc (20 sc).

Fasten off.

Round 3: With right side facing, and working in front lps only, draw up a loop of B in first sc and ch 2, 2 dc in each of next 2 sc, ch 2, sl st in next sc, [2 dc in each of next 3 sc, ch 2, sl st in next sc] 4 times, dc in same front lp of first sc; join with sl st in top of beg ch (5 petals) **(figs. E and F)**.

Fasten off.

Round 4: Push petals forward and work in back lps of each sc of Round 2, draw up a loop of C in first sc and ch 3 (counts as first tr), 2 tr in each of next 2 sc, ch 4, sl st in next sc, [3 tr in each of next 3 sc, ch 4, sl st in next sc] 4 times, tr in same back lp of first sc; join with sl st in top of beginning ch (5 large petals) **(figs. G and H)**.

Finishing

1 With right sides of the squares facing you, hold wrong sides of one single-color and one double-color granny square together. Join squares together across one side edge, as follows:

- Draw up a loop of C in corner between the squares, ch 1, working through both thicknesses, sc evenly spaced across edge. Fasten off **(fig. I)**.

- Repeat this process to join all granny squares together into a long strip, alternating the single-color and double-color squares.

2 With right sides facing, draw up a loop of C anywhere in edge of Belt, ch 1, sc evenly spaced all the way around the outer edge; join with sl st in first sc. Fasten off.

3 To begin D-ring attachment flap:

- **Row 1:** Draw up a loop of C in one of the short ends of the Belt, approximately 2 stitches from one corner, ch 1, sc in next 6 sc, turn (6 sc).

- **Rows 2 and 3:** Ch 1, sc in each sc across, turn **(fig. J)**.

- Fasten off. Place the two D-rings onto the attachment flap, then fold flap through the D-rings toward wrong side of belt. With a tapestry needle, whipstitch the flap to the edge of the belt **(fig. K)**. Stitch the flower at this spot, on the right side of belt.

tic tac toe

The pursuit of getting three-in-a-row has never been so irresistible. With this miniature game board and colorful game pieces, you'll want to play again and again.

Finished Measurements

- Game board: 5 inches
  (12.7cm) square

What You'll Need

- Basic Crochet Tool Kit, page 7
- Lion Brand Collection Cotton Bamboo (52% cotton/48% rayon; 3.5oz/100g = 245yds/224m): less than 1 ball each, (A) #098 magnolia; (B) #126 chocolate dahlia; (C) #139 hibiscus; (D) #170 gardenia **(3)**
- Crochet hook: US E-4 (3.5mm)

Gauge: Approximately 16 sts and 18 rows over 4 inches (10.2cm) of single crochet.

Always take time to check the gauge or the finished measurement of the project as provided.

Abbreviations: See page 11.

Instructions

Game Board: Outer Strips (Make 2)

To begin: With A, ch 7.

Row 1: Sc in 2nd ch from hook and in each ch across, turn (you now have 6 sc).

Rows 2–7: Ch 1, sc in each sc across, turn.

Row 8: Draw up a loop of B in first sc, ch 1, sc in each sc across, turn. Cut A **(fig. A and B)**.

Rows 9–13: Ch 1, sc in each sc across, turn.

Row 14: Draw up a loop of A in first sc, ch 1, sc in each sc across, turn. Cut B **(fig. C)**.

Rows 15–20: Ch 1, sc in each sc across, turn.

Fasten off.

Game Board: Inner Strip

Repeat Rows 1–7 with B.

Repeat Rows 8–13 with A.

Repeat Rows 14–20 with B.

Fasten off.

Game Board: Finishing

- With tapestry needle, weave in all ends of the three strips.

- With tapestry needle, whipstitch together one of the long sides of one outer strip and one of the long sides of the inner strip. Whipstitch the other long side of the inner strip to one of the long sides of the second outer strip. With tapestry needle, weave in all ends **(fig. D)**.

- With wrong side facing you, draw up a loop of A anywhere in the edge of the Game Board; ch 1, sc evenly spaced around; join with sl st in first sc. Fasten off. With tapestry needle, weave in all ends **(fig E)**.

Four-Petal Flower Game Pieces (Make 5)

Foundation Round: With C, ch 3; join with a sl st in first ch to form a ring.

Petals: *Ch 2, (dc, sl st) in loop; repeat from * 3 more times to create 4 petals. Fasten off.

With tapestry needle, weave in all ends.

Circle Game Pieces (Make 5)

With D, ch 4; join with a sl st in first ch to form a ring, ch 1. Work 10 sc in ring. Fasten off. With tapestry needle, weave in all ends.

baby's egg rattle

A pinch of uncooked rice encased in a plastic egg is all you need to make this rattle shake, shake, shake to baby's content.

Finished Measurements

- 4 inches (10.2cm) tall, 7½-inch (19cm) circumference

What You'll Need

- Basic Crochet Tool Kit, page 7
- Lion Brand Martha Stewart Crafts Cotton Hemp (65% cotton/35% hemp; 1.75oz/50g = 66yds/60m): less than 1 ball each, (A) 503 flour sack white; (B) 557 lemon drop (4)
- Crochet hook: US G-6 (4mm)
- Plastic eggs, 3⅛ inches (8cm)
- Uncooked rice, 1 teaspoon per egg
- Glue: E-6000 craft adhesive

Gauge: Approximately 10 sts and 10 rows over 4 inches (10.2cm) of single crochet.

Always take time to check the gauge or the finished measurement of the project as provided.

Abbreviations: See page 11.

Note: When using yarn made with natural fibers like hemp and cotton, you can dye the yarn in fabric dye, let it thoroughly dry, and use it to crochet. The orange egg shown on the previous page was made by dyeing A in orange fabric dye.

Stitch Guide: Puff Stitch (PS)

* Yo, insert hook in indicated stitch, yo and draw up a loop; repeat from * 3 more times, yo and draw yarn through all 9 loops on hook **(figs. A and B)**.

Instructions

Yellow Egg Rattle

Place a teaspoon of uncooked rice into the plastic egg. Glue the egg shut and wipe off any excess. Let dry **(fig. C)**.

To begin: With B, ch 3, join with sl st in first ch to form a ring.

Round 1: Ch 1, 6 sc in ring; join with sl st in first sc (6 sc).

Round 2: Ch 1, 2 sc in each sc around; join with sl st in first sc (12 sc).

Round 3: Ch 1, sc in each sc around; join with sl st in first sc.

Round 4: Ch 1, (2 sc in next sc, sc in next sc) 6 times; join with sl st in first sc (18 sc).

Round 5: Ch 1, (PS in the next sc, ch 1, sc in the next sc) 9 times; join with sl st in first st (9 PS, 9 ch-1 spaces, and 9 sc).

Round 6: Ch 1, (sc2tog, sc in next sc) 9 times; join with sl st in first st (18 sts) **(fig. D)**.

Rounds 7 and 8: Repeat Rounds 5 and 6.

Round 9: Ch 1, (sc2tog, sc in next sc) 6 times; join with sl st in first st (12 sc).

Round 10: Ch 1, sc in each sc around, join with sl st in first st.

Work the final round with the egg inside the cozy.

Round 11: Ch 1, (sc2tog) 6 times **(fig. E)**.

Fasten off, leaving a long tail.

With a tapestry needle, weave the tail back and forth at the top of the egg to stitch the rattle closed **(fig. F)**.

White Egg Rattle

Place a teaspoon of uncooked rice into the plastic egg. Glue the egg shut and wipe off any excess. Let dry.

To begin: With A, ch 3; join with sl st in first ch to form a ring.

Round 1: Ch 1, 6 sc in ring; join with sl st in first sc (you now have 6 sc).

Round 2: Ch 1, 2 sc in each sc around; join with sl st in first sc (12 sc).

Round 3: Ch 1, sc in each sc around; join with sl st in first sc.

Round 4: Ch 1, (2 sc in next sc, sc in next sc) 6 times; join with sl st in first sc (18 sc).

Round 5: Ch 2, dc in each sc around; join with sl st in first dc (18 dc).

Round 6: Ch 1, sc in each dc around; join with sl st in first sc.

Round 7: Ch 2, dc in each sc around; join with sl st in first dc **(fig. G)**.

Round 8: Ch 1, (sc2tog, 1 sc in next sc) 6 times; join with sl st in first st (12 sc).

Round 9: Ch 1, sc in each sc around; join with sl st in first sc.

Work the final round with the egg inside the cozy.

Round 10: Ch 1, (sc2tog) 6 times (6 sts).

Fasten off, leaving a long tail.

With a tapestry needle, weave the tail back and forth at the top of the egg to stitch the rattle closed.

bear ears headband

I wear this headband when I need extra help with active listening. Because the ears are crocheted with a combination of yarn and thin craft wire, they keep their shape and don't flop down—unless I fold them down on purpose!

What You'll Need

- Basic Crochet Tool Kit, page 7
- Stitch. Rock. Love. Sheep(ish) (70% acrylic/30% wool; 3oz/85g = 167yds/153m): (A) less than 1 ball, 0011 taupe(ish) **(4)**
- Headband: fabric-covered plastic, ⅝ inch (1.6cm) wide
- Black craft wire: (B) 28-gauge, 10 yards (9m)
- Crochet hook: US I-9 (5.5mm) or size needed to obtain gauge

Gauge: Use finished measurements for gauge.

Always take time to check the gauge or the finished measurement of the project as provided.

Abbreviations: See page 11.

Finished measurements

- Each ear: 2¾ x 2 inches (7 x 5.1cm)

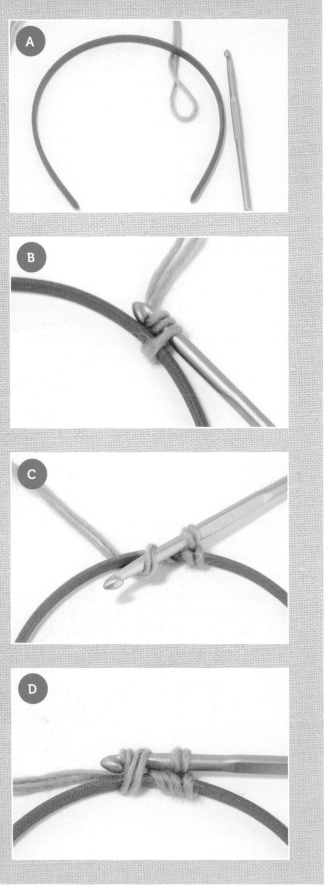

Instructions

Headband

1 Draw out enough of A to fold in half so that the folded double strand of yarn measures approximately 120 inches (305cm). Place the folded yarn at the back of the headband **(fig. A)**.

2 Beginning about 1½ inches (3.8cm) from one end of headband, bring the hook from front to back, under the headband. Place folded yarn on hook and draw the fold to the front. Bring hook over headband. Holding both strands of folded yarn together, yarn over with the double strand as shown and draw the double strand through the loop on the hook **(fig. B)**.

3 Bring the hook under the headband. Yarn over with double strand and draw loops to front **(fig. C)**.

4 Bring hook over headband, yarn over with double strand and draw through loops on hook **(fig. D)**.

5 Repeat steps 3 and 4 until 35 stitches have been worked to cover the headband **(fig. E)**.

Fasten off. With tapestry needle, weave in the ends.

Make the First Ear

Draw out enough of A to fold in half so that the folded double strand of yarn measures approximately 60 inches (152.4cm).

To begin: With right side of work facing you and with the folded double strand of A and single strand of B held together, insert the hook in the ninth stitch from the right end of the headband, yarn over and draw loops of yarn and wire through. Continue working with all strands held together for the first ear.

Row 1: Ch 1, sc in same st as join (ninth st), sc in the next 4 sts, turn (you now have 5 sc) **(fig. F)**.

Row 2: Ch 1, sc in next 5 sc, turn (5 sc).

Row 3: Ch 1, sc2tog, sc in next sc, sc2tog, turn (3 sc) **(fig. G)**.

Row 4: Ch 1, sc in next 3 sc (3 sc).

Fasten off.

Make the Second Ear

With right side of the work facing you and one double strand of yarn and single strand of craft wire held together, insert hook in thirteenth stitch from the left end of the headband, yarn over and draw loops of yarn and wire through. Continue working with all strands held together **(fig. H)**.

Repeat rows 1–4 of the first ear.

Fasten off. With tapestry needle, weave in the ends.

Finishing

Note: To finish, use a single strand of A.

With right side of the work facing you and starting from the outer base of the first ear, draw up a loop of A, ch 1.

Work 12 sc evenly spaced around outer edge of the first ear.

Sc in each st of upper portion of headband to the second ear.

Work 12 sc evenly spaced around outer edge of the second ear.

Fasten off. With a tapestry needle, weave in the ends.

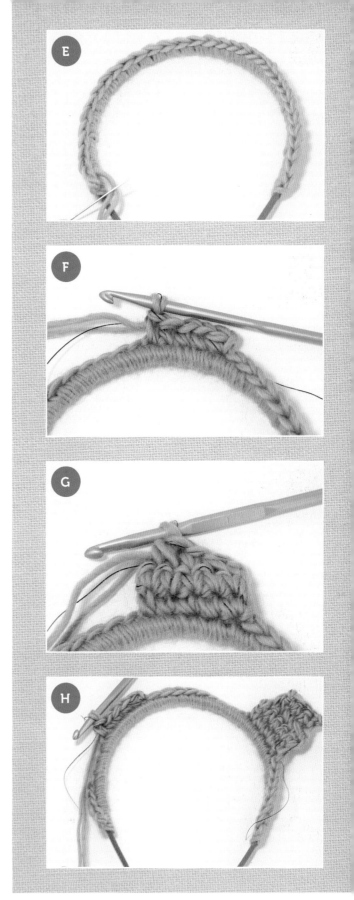

pretty paperweights

Papers on your desk won't want to stray when they can keep company with these pretty paperweights.

Finished Measurements

- Paperweight covers are adjustable and will fit rocks approximately 1–2 inches (2.5–5.1cm) in diameter.

What You'll Need

- Basic Crochet Tool Kit, page 7
- Small clean rocks or stones, 1–2 inches (2.5–5.1cm) in diameter
- Aunt Lydia's Bamboo Crochet Thread (100% bamboo; size 10; 300yds/274m): less than 1 ball each, (A) #0320 mushroom; (B) #0001 white
- Perle cotton (100% cotton; size 5): less than 1 ball each, (C) red; (D) white
- Crochet hook: US E-4 (3.5mm)
- Small white button

Gauge: Use finished measurements for gauge.

Always take time to check the gauge or the finished measurement of the project as provided.

Abbreviations: See page 11.

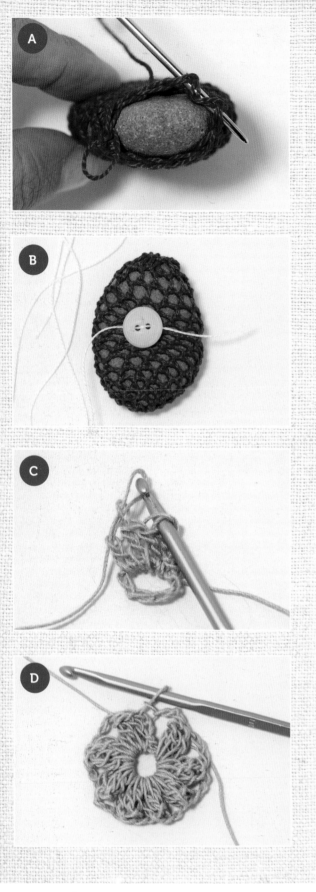

Instructions

Wrapped Button Paperweight

To begin: With C or D, ch 3; join with sl st in first ch to form a ring.

Round 1: Ch 1, 6 sc into the ring; join with sl st to form a ring (6 sc).

Round 2: 2 sc in each sc around (12 sc).

Round 3: Sc in each sc around; do not join, instead work in continuous rounds (see page 19).

Repeat Round 3 approximately 15 more times. Weave in the beginning tail with a tapestry needle. Insert the rock into the work. Fasten off, leaving a long tail. Weave tail through stitches of last round and pull to gather **(fig. A)**. Weave in end securely. Thread a button with D, wrap and tie it to the paperweight **(fig. B)**.

Tip

Place a safety pin or stitch marker at the beginning of each round if you want to keep precise track of the number of continuous rounds. However, it's okay if you lose track or decide to stop in the middle of a round, based on how well the crochet fits the rock.

Stitch Guide: Popcorn Stitch (PC)

Work 4 dc stitches in the indicated stitch or space, drop loop from hook, insert hook in top of first dc of the 4-dc group and back into dropped loop. Draw the loop through the loop on hook **(fig. C)**.

Popcorn Petals Paperweight

To begin: With A or B, ch 6; join with sl st in first ch to form a ring.

Round 1: Sl st in ring, ch 3, 3 dc in ring, drop loop from hook, insert hook in top of beg ch-3 and back into dropped loop, draw loop through the loop on hook (beg PC made), ch 3, (PC in ring, ch 3) 7 times; join with sl st in top of beg ch-3 (you now have 8 PC and 8 ch-3 sps) **(fig. D)**.

Round 2: Ch 1, sc in first ch-3 sp, (ch 4, sc in next ch-3 sp) 7 times, ch 4; join with sl st in first sc (8 sc and 8 ch-4 sps) **(fig. E)**.

Round 3: Ch 2 (does not count as a st), dc in each ch and sc around; join with sl st in top of beg ch-2 (40 dc). Weave in beginning tail with a tapestry needle **(fig. F)**.

Round 4: Ch 1, sc in next dc, *skip next dc, sc in next dc; repeat from * around to last dc, skip last dc; join with sl st in first sc (20 sc) **(fig. G)**.

Note: About halfway through this round, slip the rock into the work and finish the round. Repeat Round 4 as many more times as needed, as you crochet with the cozy on the rock. Fasten off, leaving a long tail. Weave tail through stitches of last round and pull to gather. Weave in end securely.

camera strap cover + lens cap pouch

In a sea of cameras, yours will be the only one with this stylish strap cover. The coordinating pouch will help you keep track of the frequently wayward lens cap.

Finished Measurements

- For strap cover: 26½ x 2 inches (67.3 x 5.1cm)
- For pouch (folded and buttoned shut): 4¼ x 3½ inches (10.8 x 8.9cm)

What You'll Need

- Basic Crochet Tool Kit, page 7
- Lion Brand Cotton Ease (50% cotton/50% acrylic; 3.5oz/100g = 207yds/188m): less than 1 ball each, (A) #122 taupe; (B) #123 seaspray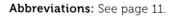
- Crochet hook: US G-6 (4mm) or size needed to obtain gauge

Gauge: Approximately 12 sts and 16 rows over 4 inches (10.2cm) of single crochet

Always take time to check the gauge or the finished measurement of the project as provided.

Abbreviations: See page 11.

Note: This camera strap cover and pouch were made to fit the strap of the Canon 30D DSLR camera that measures 1½ x 26 inches (3.8 x 66cm). Depending on the measurements of your camera strap, you may need to adjust the number of chain stitches you begin with, and the number of rows worked.

Instructions

Strap (Make 2)

To begin: With A, ch 7.

Row 1: Sc in 2nd ch from hook and in each ch across, turn (you now have 6 sc).

Row 2: Ch 1, sc in each sc, turn.

Repeat Row 2 until the piece measures the length of the main fabric portion of your camera strap, turn.

Pointed Edge Row 1: Draw up a loop of B, ch 1, sc in each sc across, turn (6 sc). Cut A.

Pointed Edge Row 2: Ch 1, sc in each sc across, turn.

Pointed Edge Row 3: Ch 1, sc2tog, sc in next 2 sc, sc2tog, turn (4 sc).

Pointed Edge Row 4: Ch 1, sc in each sc across, turn.

Pointed Edge Row 5: Ch 1, [sc2tog] twice (2 sc) **(fig. A)**.

Fasten off.

Repeat Pointed Edge Rows 1–5 on the opposite end of the strap.

Sandwich the camera strap between the two crocheted pieces and whipstitch all edges closed.

Lens Cap Pouch Body

To begin: With B, ch 14.

Row 1: Sc in 2nd ch from hook and in each ch across, turn (13 sc).

Rows 2–24: Ch 1, sc in each sc across, turn.

Fasten off.

Lens Cap Pouch Flap

Row 25: Draw up a loop of A in first sc, ch 1, sc in each sc across, turn (13 sc).

Row 26: Ch 1, sc in each sc across, turn.

Row 27: Ch 1, sc2tog, sc in next 9 sc, sc2tog, turn (11 sc).

Row 28: Ch 1, sc in each sc across, turn.

Row 29: Ch 1, sc2tog, sc in next 7 sc, sc2tog, turn (9 sc).

Row 30: Ch 1, sc in each sc across, turn.

Row 31: Ch 1, sc2tog, sc in next 5 sc, sc2tog, turn (7 sc).

Row 32: Ch 1, sc in each sc across, turn.

Row 33: Ch 1, sc2tog, sc in next sc, ch 1 and sk next sc (buttonhole made), sc in next sc, sc2tog, turn (4 sc and 1 ch-1 sp) **(fig B)**.

Row 34: Ch 1, sc in each st and ch-1 sp across, turn.

Row 35: Ch 1, sc in each sc across, turn.

Fasten off.

Fold the bottom edge up to the start of the flap and whipstitch the sides together to form body of the pouch **(fig. C)**.

Lens Cap Pouch Circle Button

To begin: With B, ch 3; join with sl st in first ch to form ring.

Round 1: Ch 1, work 10 sc in center of ring; join with sl st in first sc. Fasten off, leaving a long tail. Use tail to sew the circle button to the center front of the pouch, aligned with the buttonhole on the pouch flap.

Lens Cap Pouch Back Loop

To begin: With B, ch 10.

Row 1: Sc in 2nd ch from hook and in each ch across, turn (9 sc).

Rows 2–11: Ch 1, sc in each sc across, turn.

Fasten off.

Sandwich the camera strap between the pouch and back loop. Place the loop on the back side of the pouch so that the short sides of the loop align with the short sides of the pouch, and the long sides of the loop are centered across the long sides of the pouch. Taking care not to sew through the camera strap, use tails to sew the long sides of the loop to the pouch **(fig. D)**.

With tapestry needle, weave in all ends.

embellished knee-highs

To add flirty fun to your knee-highs, a touch of crochet trim and dangly flowers are all you need.

What You'll Need

- Basic Crochet Tool Kit, page 7
- Aunt Lydia's Bamboo Crochet Thread (100% viscose from bamboo; size 10; 300 yds/274m): (A) less than 1 ball, #0275 coral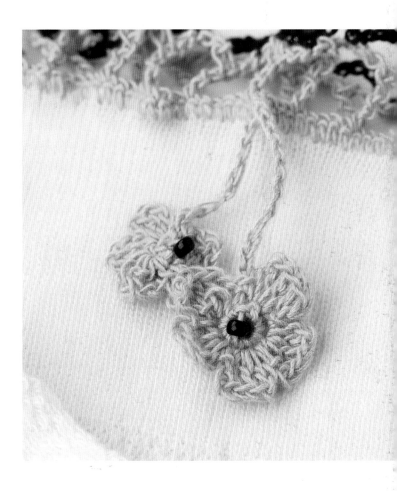
- DMC Perle Cotton, (100% cotton; size 8; 10g = 95yds): (B) less than 1 ball, #0310 black
- 1 pair of off-white knee-high socks with fine rib top edge
- Steel crochet hook: US 8 (1.5mm)
- 4 small seed beads: black

Gauge: Width of trim measures about ¾ inch (1.9cm).

Always take time to check the gauge or the finished measurement of the project as provided.

Abbreviations: See page 11.

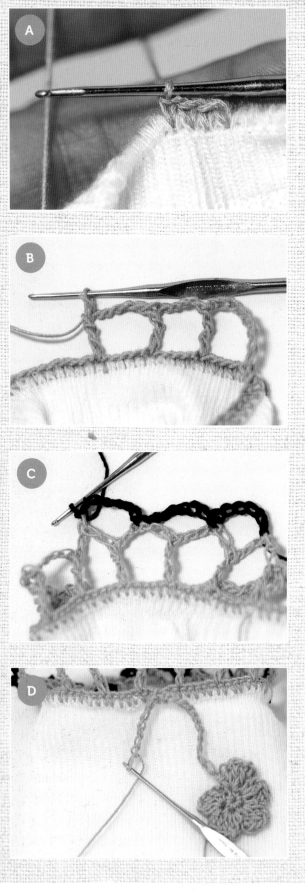

Instructions

Cuff Embellishment

To begin: Hold the sock so the inside is facing you. With A, draw up a loop through one of the ribs at the top edge of the sock, ch 1.

Round 1: Sc in each rib around; join with sl st in first sc **(fig. A)**.

Note: For this standard-size sock, 98 sc were worked.

Round 2: Ch 9 (counts as tr, ch 5), sk next 4 sc, tr in next sc, *ch 5, sk next 4 sc, tr in next sc; repeat from * around, ch 5; join with sl st in 4th ch of beginning ch. Note: The number of sc skipped at the end of Round 2 will vary, depending on the number of sc that were worked around the top of the sock **(fig. B)**.

Fasten off.

Round 3: Draw up a loop of B in the 3rd ch of one of the ch-5 spaces of Round 2, *ch 5, sl st in 3rd ch of next ch-5 space of Round 2; repeat from * around, ch 5; join with sl st in base of first ch-5. Fasten off **(fig. C)**.

With tapestry needle, weave in ends.

Dangling Flowers

Foundation Round for Large Flower: With A, ch 2, work 5 sc in 2nd ch from hook; join with sl st in first sc (5 sc).

Large Petals: [Ch 2, (3 dc, ch 2, sl st) in next sc] 5 times to create 5 petals.

Dangle Cord: Ch 12, sl st in sc on outer side center of sock, ch 10 **(fig. D)**.

Foundation Round for Small Flower: Work 5 sc in 2nd ch from hook; join with sl st in first sc (5 sc).

Small Petals: [Ch 2, (dc, ch 2, sl st) in next sc] 5 times to create 5 petals.

Fasten off. Repeat instructions to crochet second sock.

With hand embroidery needle and A, sew small black beads to the centers of both flowers on both socks. Fasten off. With tapestry needle, weave in ends.

skinny scalloped scarf

Because this scarf is made with super chunky yarns, it can be worked up very fast. You'll want to make several as gifts for all the skinny scarf lovers in your life.

Finished Measurements

- 33 x 2½ inches (83.8 x 6.4cm)

What You'll Need

- Basic Crochet Tool Kit, page 7
- Bernat Roving (80% acrylic/20% wool; 3.5oz/100g = 120yds/109m): (A) less than 1 ball, #00098 low tide **⑤**
- Loops & Threads Cozy Wool (50% acrylic/50% wool; 4.5oz/127g = 90yds/82m): (B) less than 1 ball, granite **⑥**
- Lily Sugar 'n Cream (100% cotton: 2.5oz/70g = 120yds/109m): (C) less than 1 ball, #00001 white **④**
- Crochet hook: US J-10 (6.0mm) or size needed to obtain gauge

Gauge: Two scallops measure approximately 1½ inches (3.8cm) tall. One scallop measures about 1 inch (2.5cm) wide.

Always take time to check the gauge or the finished measurement of the project as provided.

Abbreviations: See page 11

Instructions

To begin: With A, ch 3.

Closed Scallops: *3 dc in 3rd ch from hook, ch 3; repeat from * until you have approximately 46 scallops, or to desired length. Fasten off. If necessary, untwist the piece so that all beginning chains are across one long edge and all 3-dc groups are stacked one on top of each other **(figs. A and B)**.

Open Scallops (to begin): Draw up a loop of B in one end of the long straight edge (the edge opposite the beginning ch-3's) of the closed scallops, ch 1, work 3 sc in edge of each scallop across long edge, turn (you now have 138 sc) **(fig. C)**.

Open Scallops (to finish): (Ch 6, sk next 2 sc, sl st in next sc) 45 times, ch 6, sk next 2 sc, sl st in final sc. Fasten off **(fig. D)**.

White Accent: With approximately 66 inches (167.6cm) of C and a tapestry needle, weave C in and out, along the center of the scarf. Fasten off. Weave in all ends **(fig. E)**.

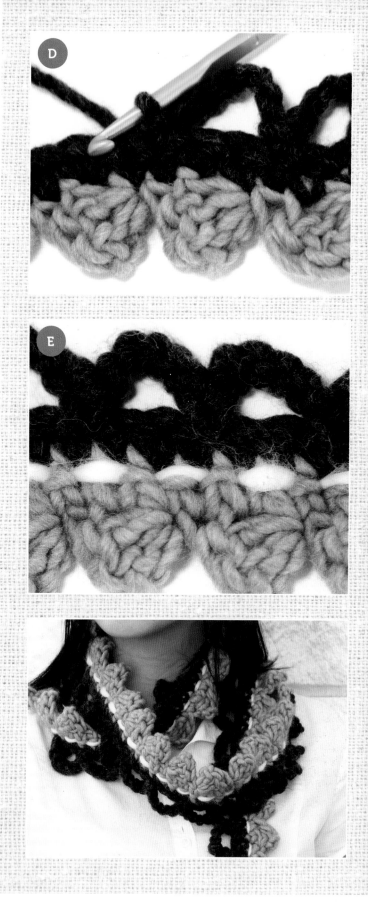

soap saver + washcloth

Instead of throwing away your leftover soap pieces, put them in this clever soap saver to use in the shower or bathtub. The hemp yarn will lather up the soap and help exfoliate every time you use it. In combination with the matching washcloth, this duo makes a wonderful gift.

Finished Measurements

- For soap saver: 4½ x 4 inches (11.4 x 10.2cm)
- For washcloth: 5 x 6¾ inches (12.7 x 17.1cm)

What You'll Need

- Basic Crochet Tool Kit, page 7
- Worsted Weight Hemp Yarn (100% hemp; 1.1lb/500g = 425yds/392m): (A) less than 1 ball (4)
- Baker's Twine, 10-ply (100% cotton; 300yds/274.3m): (B) less than 1 spool, red & white
- Crochet hook: US I-9 (5.5mm)

Gauge: Soap Saver: Approximately 10 sts and 12 rows over 4 inches (10.2cm) of single crochet. Washcloth: Approximately 9 sts and 12 rows over 4 inches (10.2cm) of single crochet

Always take time to check the gauge or the finished measurement of the project as provided.

Abbreviations: See page 11.

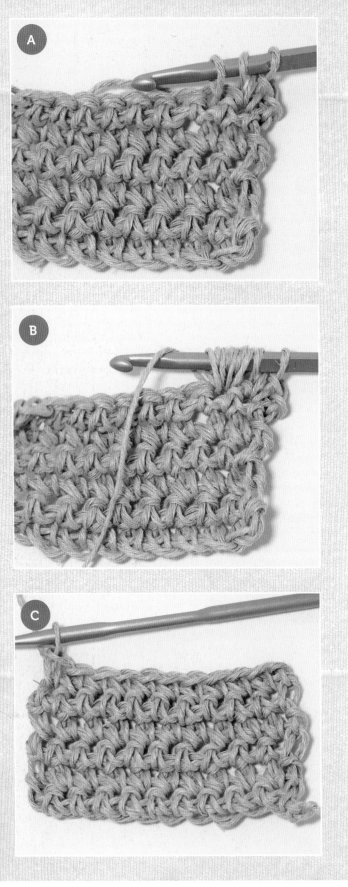

Stitch Guide: Puff Stitch (PS)

* Yo, insert hook in indicated stitch, yo and draw up a loop **(fig. A)**; repeat from * 3 times. yo and draw yarn through all 9 loops on hook **(fig. B)**.

Instructions

Soap Saver: Top Edge

To begin: With A, ch 11.

Row 1: Sc in 2nd ch from hook and in each ch across, turn (you now have 10 sc).

Rows 2–6: Ch 1, sc in each sc across, turn **(fig. C)**.

Soap Saver: Body

Row 7: Ch 1, sc in first sc, *PS in next sc, ch 1, sc in next sc; repeat from * 3 times, sc in last sc, turn (6 sc, 4 PS, and 4 ch-1 sp) **(fig.D)**.

Row 8: Ch 1, sc in first 2 sc, *sc2tog, sc in next st; repeat from * 3 more times, turn (10 sts).

Row 9: Ch 1, sc in first 2 sc, *PS in next sc, ch 1, sc in next sc; repeat from * 3 times, turn (6 sc, 4 PS, and 4 ch-1 sp).

Row 10: Ch 1, sc in first sc, *sc2tog, sc in next st; repeat from * 3 times, sc in last st, turn (10 sts).

Rows 11–26: Repeat rows 7–10 4 more times.

Soap Saver: Outer Flap

Rows 27–32: Ch 1, sc in each sc across, turn.

Fasten off **(fig. E)**.

Fold the outer flap toward the backside, and fold up the body in half toward the front so that the top edge aligns with the outer flap folds **(fig. F)**.

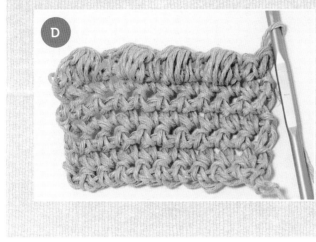

With A and a tapestry needle, whipstitch the sides and the outer flap together **(fig.G)**. Weave in the ends.

Note: Insert leftover soap pieces into the main pocket of the soap saver and then flip the outer flap over toward the front.

Three-Petal Flower

Foundation Round: With B, ch 2, work 5 sc in 2nd ch from the hook; join with a sl st in first sc (you now have 5 sc).

Petals: *Ch 2, (2 dc, ch 2, sl st) in next sc; repeat from * 2 more times to create 3 petals; leave remaining sts unworked. Fasten off, leaving a long tail for sewing the flower to the outer flap. With a tapestry needle, sew the flower to the outer flap of the Soap Saver.

Washcloth

To begin: With A, ch 12.

Row 1: Sc in 2nd ch from hook and in each ch across, turn (11 sc).

Rows 2–19: Ch 1, sc in each sc across, turn.

Fasten off.

With wrong side facing you, draw up a loop of B anywhere in the edge of the washcloth; ch 1, sc evenly spaced around; join with sl st in first sc.

Fasten off. With a tapestry needle, weave in all ends.

lemonade coasters + glass cozies

With these cheerful coasters and glass cozies, all you need is ice cold lemonade and a fun treat to get the party started.

Finished Measurements

- For coasters: 4½ x 4 inches (11.4 x 10.2cm)

What You'll Need

- Basic Crochet Tool Kit, page 7
- Aunt Lydia's Bamboo Crochet Thread (100% viscose from bamboo; size 10; 300yds/274m): (A) less than 1 ball, #0705 pure pink
- DMC Baroque Crochet Cotton (100% cotton; size 10; 416yds/380m); (B) less than 1 ball, white
- The Twinery Baker's Twine, 4-ply (100% cotton; 240yds): (C) less than 1 spool, yellow & white.
- Gütermann elastic thread (64% polyester, 36% polyurethane; 10m): (D) less than 1 spool, white
- Crochet hook: US B-1 (2.25mm)

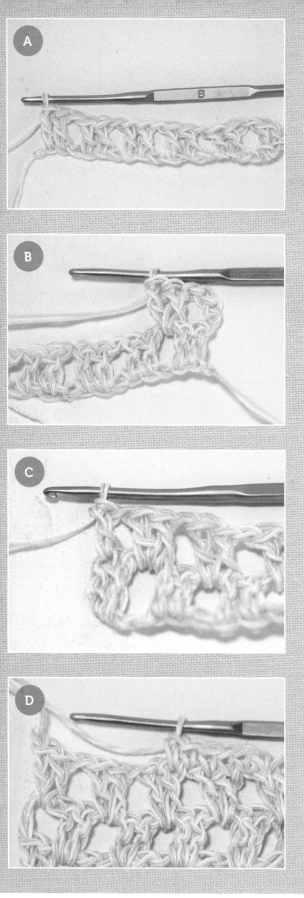

Gauge: Approximately 18 sts and 7 rows over 4 inches (10.2cm) of double crochet, ch 1 pattern.

Always take time to check the gauge or the finished measurement of the project as provided.

Abbreviations: See page 11.

Instructions

Coaster

To begin: With one strand each of A and B held together, ch 19.

Row 1: Dc in 4th ch from hook (beginning ch counts as dc), (ch 1, sk next ch, dc in next 2 ch) 5 times, turn (12 dc and 5 ch-1 sps) **(fig. A)**.

Row 2: Ch 4 (counts as dc and ch 1), (2 dc in next ch-1 sp, ch 1) 5 times, dc in 3rd ch of turning ch, turn (12 dc and 6 ch-1 sps) **(figs. B and C)**.

Row 3: Ch 3, dc in next ch-1 sp, ch 1, (2 dc in next ch-1 sp, ch 1) 4 times, ch 1, 2 dc in last ch-sp, turn.

Rows 4–7: Repeat last 2 rows 2 times. Fasten off.

Trim: With RS facing, draw up a loop of C anywhere in edge of the coaster, ch 1, sc evenly spaced around; join with sl st in first sc. *Ch 3, sl st in same sc as join, sk next sc, *(sc, ch 3, sl st) in next sc, sk next sc; repeat from * around; join with sl st in base of beginning ch-3 **(figs. D and E)**.

Fasten off. With tapestry needle, weave in ends.

Stitch Guide: Join with a sc

Place a slip knot on the hook, insert the hook in the indicated st and draw up a loop, yarn over and draw through both loops on hook (sc made).

Glass Cozy

Note: Measure the circumference and create enough chain stitches to fit the glass very snugly or it may slide off. The glass used here had a circumference of 10½ inches (26.7cm), for which the following stitches were made:

To begin: Leaving long beginning tails, with one strand each of A, B, and D held together, ch 49.

Row 1: Sc in 2nd ch from hook, sc in each ch across, turn (you now have 48 sc).

Row 2: Ch 1, sc in each sc across, fasten off A, B, and D, leaving a long tail.

Row 3: Draw up a loop of C in first sc, ch 1, sc in same sc and all sc across, turn **(fig. F)**.

Row 4: Ch 3, sl st in first sc, sk next sc, sc in next sc, *ch 3, sl st in same sc, sk next sc, sc in next sc; repeat from * across **(fig. G)**.

Fasten off. Use beginning tails to whipstitch edges of the cozy together. With tapestry needle, weave in all remaining ends. Slip the cozy onto the glass.

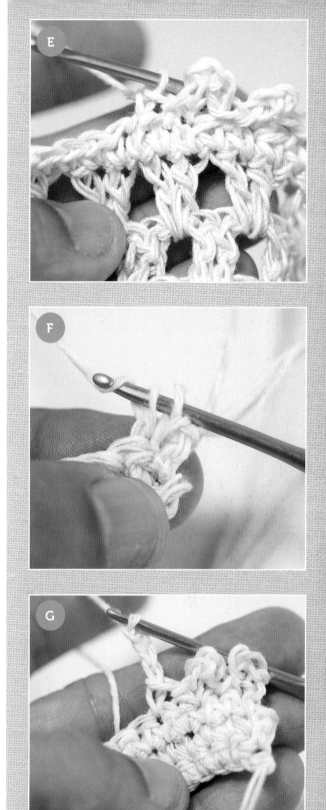

four-fish mobile

In a baby's or toddler's room, this four-fish mobile will add lots of color, movement, and cheer.

Finished Measurements

- For each fish: 4½ x 3 inches (11.4 x 7.6cm)

What You'll Need

- Basic Crochet Tool Kit, page 7

- Stitch. Rock. Love. Sheep(ish) (70% acrylic/30% wool; 3oz/85g = 167yds/153m): less than 1 ball each, (A) #0020 chartreush(ish), (B) #0007 hot pink(ish), (C) #0017 turquoise(ish), (D) #0012 yellow(ish) (4)

- DMC Perle Cotton 5 (100% cotton; 5g = 27.3yds/24m): (E) less than 1 ball, 0310 black

- Crochet hook: US D-3 (3.25mm)

- Hand embroidery needle

- Polyester fiberfill, 1 ounce

- Wooden embroidery hoop: 6 inches (15.2cm)

- Black spray paint

- Invisible nylon thread: 3 yards (2.7m), divided and cut into 4 pieces

- Black craft wire: 3 yards (2.7m), divided and cut into 4 pieces

Gauge: Use finished measurements for gauge.

Always take time to check the gauge or the finished measurement of the project as provided.

Abbreviations: See page 11.

Note: Two fish-shaped pieces are made for each fish. Each pair is embroidered with French knots for eyes and then crocheted together to form one fish.

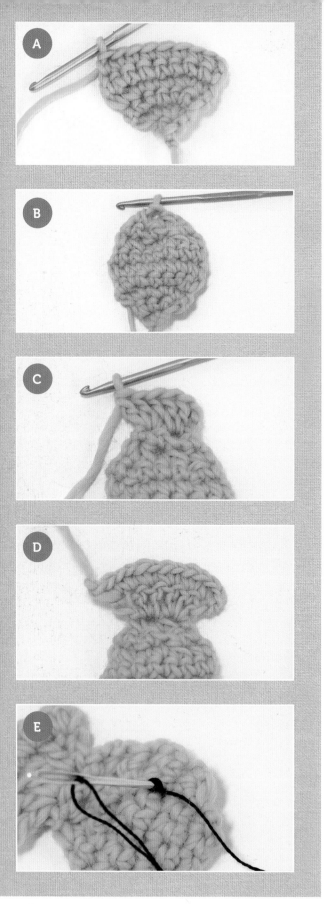

Instructions

To begin: With D, ch 2, work 2 sc in 2nd ch from the hook, turn.

Row 1: Ch 1, 2 sc in each sc, turn (you now have 4 sc).

Row 2: Ch 1, sc in next sc, 2 sc in each of next 2 sc, sc in next sc, turn (6 sc).

Row 3: Ch 1, sc in next sc, 2 sc in next sc, sc in next 2 sc, 2 sc in next sc, sc in next sc, turn (8 sc) **(fig. A)**.

Rows 4 and 5: Ch 1, sc in each sc across, turn.

Row 6: Ch 1, sc in next sc, sc2tog, sc in next 2 sc, sc2tog, sc in next sc, turn (6 sc).

Row 7: Ch 1, sc in first sc, (sc2tog) 2 times, sc in next sc, turn (4 sc).

Row 8: Ch 1, (sc2tog) 2 times, turn (2 sc) **(fig. B)**.

Row 9: Ch 2 (counts as first dc), 2 dc in first sc, 3 dc in last sc, turn (6 dc) **(fig. C)**.

Row 10: Ch 1, 2 sc in each dc across, 2 sc in top of beginning ch-2 (12 sc).

Fasten off **(fig. D)**. Repeat instructions to make second fish shape with D.

With E, embroider a French knot eye on the outside of each fish shape. With a tapestry needle, weave in all ends **(figs. E and F)**.

Hold the two fish shapes together, and draw up a loop of yarn anywhere in edge of the fish. Ch 1, working through both thicknesses, sc evenly spaced around, leaving a small 1-inch (2.5cm) opening.

Stuff with polyester fiberfill through the opening **(fig. G)**. Continue with sc evenly across the opening: join with sl st in first sc. Fasten off. Repeat instructions to make three more fish, one with A, one with B, and one with C.

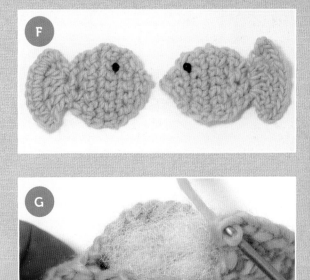

Mobile

1 Paint a wooden embroidery hoop with black spray paint and let dry.

2 Thread invisible nylon thread at the top edge of a fish so that it is doubled **(fig. H)** and tie the ends to the inner portion of the painted wooden embroidery hoop. Allow each fish to hang at slightly different heights.

3 Join the inner and outer portions of the hoop together, securing the nylon threads, and tighten with the attached screw.

4 Twist one end of each piece of black craft wire around the embroidery hoop at evenly spaced locations. Twist the opposite ends of the wires together at the top to create a loop for hanging **(figs. I and J)**.

French Knot

Perfect for making eyes, or whenever you want to add interest or texture.

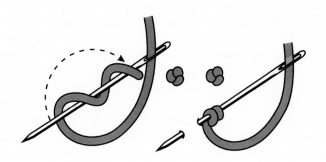

finger puppets

It's the little things like ears, snout, and scallop trim that make these finger puppets the cutest around.

Finished Measurements

- Each puppet: Approximately 2 inches (5.1cm) in circumference

What You'll Need

- Basic Crochet Tool Kit, page 7
- Aunt Lydia's Bamboo Crochet Thread (100% viscose from bamboo, size 10; 300yds/274m): less than 1 ball each, (A) #320 mushroom; (B) #001 white; (C) #705 pure pink
- DMC Perle Cotton 5 (100% cotton; 5g = 27yds/25m): (D) less than 1 ball, 0310 black
- 4 small black seed beads
- 2 small oval faceted beads
- Hand embroidery needle
- Black thread
- Crochet hook: US B-1 (2.25mm)

Gauge: Use finished size for gauge.

Always take time to check the gauge or the finished measurement of the project as provided.

Abbreviations: See page 11.

Instructions

Rabbit Body

To begin: With A, ch 2, 6 sc in 2nd ch from hook; join with sl st in first sc (you now have 6 sc).

Round 1: Ch 1, 2 sc in each sc (12 sc) **(fig A)**.

Additional Rounds: Work in continuous rounds with 1 sc in each sc without joining the rounds, until the work fits the top segment of your finger. Fasten off.

Scallop Round: Draw up a loop of B in next sc, ch 2, 2 dc in same sc, sc in next sc, *3 dc in next sc, sc in next sc; repeat from * around; join with sl st in top of beginning ch **(figs. B, C, and D)**.

Fasten off. With tapestry needle, weave in all ends.

Rabbit Ears and Face

1 Fold enough of A so that the double strand is approximately 24 inches (61cm).

2 With the double strand, *ch 7, sc in 2nd ch from hook, hdc in each of next 5 ch; repeat from * to make the second ear. Fasten off **(figs. E, F, and G)**.

3 With tapestry needle and thread tails from the ears, sew the ears to the top of the rabbit's head. Weave in all ends.

With hand embroidery needle and black thread, sew seed beads for eyes. Use D to embroider a small straight stitch for the nose.

Pig Body

With C, create the Pig Body by following the directions for the Rabbit Body.

Pig Ears and Face

1 Fold enough of C so that the double strand is approximately 24 inches (61cm).

2 Ears: With the double strand, draw up a loop at top of pig's head (slightly to one side), ch 3, sc in same sp as the first loop, ch 1, sc around next st at top of pig's head, ch 3, sc in same space. Fasten off **(figs. H, I, J, and K)**.

3 Snout: With a double strand of C, ch 2, 5 sc in 2nd ch from hook; join with sl st in first sc.

4 With tapestry needle and thread tails from the snout, sew the snout to front of pig's face.

5 With hand embroidery needle and D, make 2 French knots (see page 77) on the snout. With black thread, sew two seed beads for eyes. Weave in all ends.

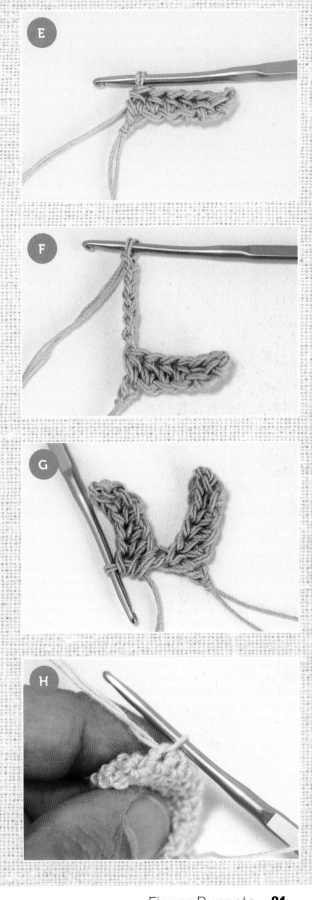

Panda Body

With B, create the Panda Body by following the directions for the Rabbit Body. Work the Scallop Round with D.

Panda Ears and Face

1 With D, ch 2, 4 sc in 2nd ch from hook. Fasten off. Repeat this step to make a second ear (fig L).

2 With tapestry needle and thread tails from the ears, sew the ears to the top of the head.

3 With a hand embroidery needle and black thread, sew the two oval beads for the eyes. Use D to embroider small straight stitches for the nose and mouth. Weave in all ends.

this little house

Crochet this cozy little house with different colors and embellishments to suit celebrations and seasons throughout the year. These are so much fun, you might want to crochet a cozy little village.

What You'll Need

- Basic Crochet Tool Kit, page 7

- Lion Brand Collection Cotton Bamboo (52% cotton/48% rayon; 3.5oz/100g = 24yds/224m): less than 1 ball each, (A) #170 gardenia; (B) #102 cherry blossom; (C) #098 magnolia (3)

- Silver craft wire: 28-gauge, (D) 10 yards (9.1m)

- Crochet Hook: US F-5 (3.75mm)

Gauge: Approximately 16 sts and 13 rows over 4 inches (10.2cm) of single crochet

Always take time to check the gauge or the finished measurement of the project as provided.

Abbreviations: See page 11.

Instructions

Squares (Make 2)

To begin: With one strand each of A and D held together, ch 11.

Row 1: Sc in 2nd ch from hook and in each ch across, turn (you now have 10 sc).

Rows 2–8: Ch 1, sc in each sc across, turn.

Fasten off. With tapestry needle weave in all ends.

Squares with a point (Make 2)

To begin: With one strand each of A and D held together, ch 11.

Row 1: Sc in 2nd ch from hook and in each ch across, turn (10 sc).

Rows 2–8: Ch 1, sc in each sc across, turn. Fasten off A.

Row 9: Draw up a loop of one strand each of B and D held together, ch 1, sc in the same space **(fig. A)** and in each sc across, turn.

Row 10: Ch 1, sc2tog, sc in next 6 sc, sc2tog, turn (8 sc).

Row 11: Ch 1, sc2tog, sc in next 4 sc, sc2tog, turn (6 sc).

Row 12: Ch 1, sc2tog, sc in next 2 sc, sc2tog, turn (4 sc).

Row 13: Ch 1, sc2tog twice, turn (2 sc).

Row 14: Ch 1, sc2tog (1sc) **(fig. B)**.

Fasten off.

Roof

To begin roof: With one strand each of B and D held together, ch 12.

Row 1: Sc in 2nd ch from hook and in each ch across, turn (11 sc).

Rows 1–18: Ch 1, sc in each sc across, turn.

Fasten off. With tapestry needle, weave in all ends.

Heart

To begin heart: With C, ch 3; join with sl st in first ch to form a ring.

Round 1: Ch 3, (2 dc, 3 sc) in ring, ch 1, dc in ring, ch 1, (3 sc, 2 dc) in ring, ch 2, sl st in ring.

Fasten off.

Finishing

1 Lay out the squares side by side: one plain square, then one square with a point (pointing up), one plain square, and the remaining square with a point (pointing up).

2 With A, whipstitch the squares together along the side edges. Stitch the first and last sides together to make the house shape.

3 Place the roof on top of the house, making a fold in the pointed center. With B, attach the roof by whip stitching along the edges of the squares.

4 With tapestry needle and C, sew the heart onto the center front of the house. Weave in all ends.

Tip

The crocheted house can be made bigger or smaller by increasing or decreasing the number of beginning chain stitches for the squares, squares with points, and roof, in same amounts.

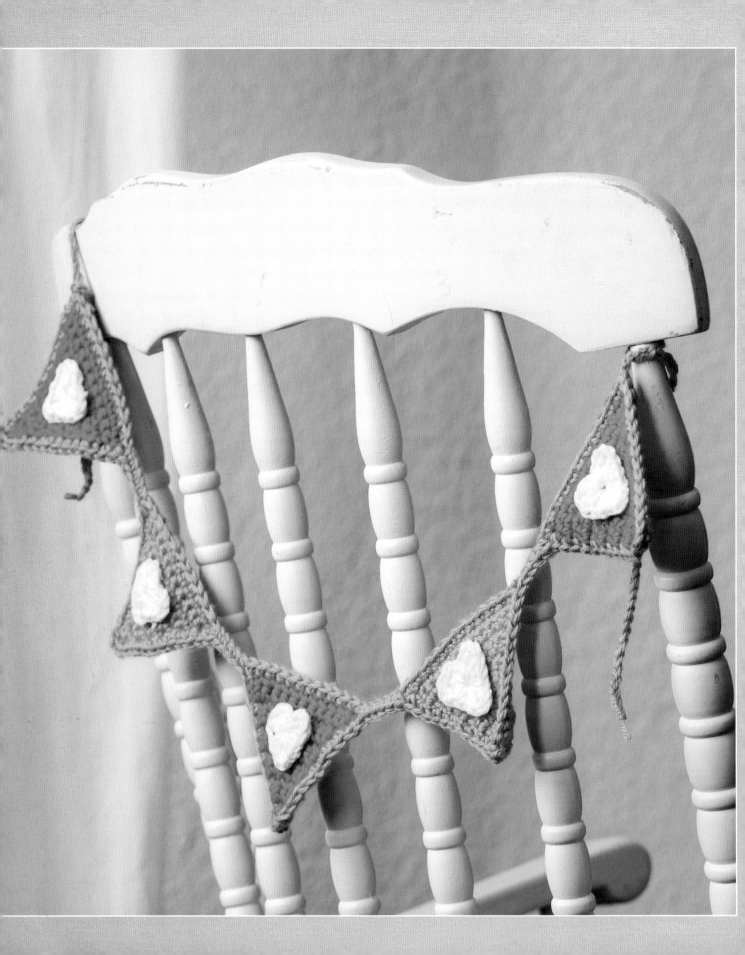

bunting with hearts

Brighten up a nursery, a mantle, or an entryway with this simple bunting with sweet little hearts.

Finished Measurements

- Each triangle: 3½ x 3 inches (8.9 x 7.6cm)
- Bunting with five triangles: 49 inches (124.5cm) long

What You'll Need

- Basic Crochet Tool Kit, page 7

- Stitch. Rock. Love. Sheep(ish) (70% acrylic/30% wool; 3oz/85g = 167yds/153m): less than 1 ball each, (A) #0017 turquoise(ish), (B) #0020 chartreuse(ish) **(4)**

- Lily Cotton Sugar 'n Cream (100% cotton; 2.5oz/70g = 120yds/109m): (C) less than 1 ball, #25001 powder **(4)**

- Crochet hook: US E-4 (3.5mm)

Gauge: Use finished measurements for gauge.

Always take time to check the gauge or the finished measurement of the project as provided.

Abbreviations: See page 11.

Instructions

Triangles (make 3 with A and 2 with B)

To begin: Ch 2, 2 sc in 2nd ch from hook, turn (you now have 2 sc) **(fig. A)**.

Row 1: Ch 1, sc in each sc, turn.

Row 2: Ch 1, 2 sc in each sc, turn (4 sc).

Row 3: Ch 1, sc in each sc, turn.

Row 4: Ch 1, 2 sc in first sc, sc in each of next 2 sc, 2 sc in next sc, turn (6 sc).

Row 5: Ch 1, sc in each sc, turn.

Row 6: Ch 1, 2 sc in first sc, sc in each sc across to last sc, 2 sc in last sc, turn (8 sc).

Rows 7–10: Repeat Rows 5 and 6 twice (12 sc at the end of Row 10) **(fig. B)**.

Row 11: Ch 1, sc in each sc, turn.

Fasten off. With tapestry needle, weave in all ends.

Hearts (make 5)

To make: With C, ch 3, join with sl st in first ch to form a ring, ch 3, (2 dc, 3 sc) in ring, ch 1, dc in ring, ch 1, (3 sc, 2 dc) in ring, ch 2, sl st in ring **(fig. C, D, and E)**.

Fasten off.

With tapestry needle and C, sew one heart on each triangle and weave in all ends.

Finishing

To begin: With B, ch 50.

Join the triangles: Sc in each sc across top edge of first A triangle, ch 5 **(fig. F)**. Sc in each sc across top edge of first B triangle, ch 5. Continue in this way until all triangles are joined, ch 50 **(fig. G)**. Fasten off.

Finish the lower edges: With right side facing, draw up a loop of B in top corner of last joined triangle, ch 1. Sc evenly along the two remaining edges of this triangle. Sc in each of the 5 ch stitches. Repeat steps until all edges of triangles and chain links have been worked. Fasten off. With tapestry needle, weave in all ends.

upcycled chair cushion

Got old bed sheets? Tear them into strips and join them to make super chunky upcycled yarn that can be crocheted into a chic chair cushion.

Finished Measurements

- 16½ inches (4.9cm) diameter

What You'll Need

- Basic Crochet Tool Kit, page 7
- Patterned twin-size flat bed sheet: (A)
- Solid twin size flat bed sheet: (B)
- Crochet hook: US N/P-15 (10mm)

Gauge: Approximately 5 sts and 5 rows over 4½ inches (11.4cm) of single crochet.

Always take time to check the gauge or the finished measurement of the project as provided.

Abbreviations: See page 11.

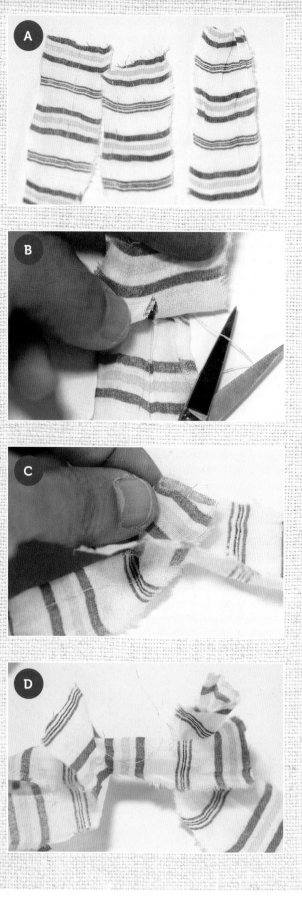

Instructions

Upcycled Bed Sheet Yarn

1 Cut a slit in the middle of one of the long sides of the sheet and rip the sheet in half. Working with halves of the bed sheet will allow you to handle the strip-making process with greater ease. Trim and rip to remove all hemmed edges on both halves.

2 Working with one of the halves, cut a slit in one of the short sides about 1 inch (2.5cm) from the edge and rip to create a 1-inch (2.5cm) wide strip. Repeat this process until both halves have been completely ripped into strips **(fig. A)**.

3 Fold under a short end of one strip about 2 inches (5.1cm). Cut a slit into the center of the folded end, about ¼ inch (.6cm) long **(fig. B)**. When you unfold the strip, you'll have a ½-inch (1.3 cm) opening. Repeat to cut slits in both short ends of all the strips.

4 To join the strips:
- Thread one end of a strip (strip 1) into the slit at one end of another strip (strip 2), from bottom to top **(fig. C)**.
- Thread the opposite end of strip 1 into the slit of the threaded end of strip 1 **(fig. D)**.
- Pull the strips so that they become snug and joined **(fig. E)**.
- Repeat with new strips until all strips are joined into a large ball of upcycled bed sheet yarn.

Chair Cushion

To begin: With A, ch 3; join with sl st in first ch to form a ring.

Round 1: Ch 1, 6 sc in ring, join with a sl st in first sc (you now have 6 sc).

Note: Place marker to indicate last stitch of round. Move marker to new last stitch as each round is completed.

Round 2: Ch 1, 2 sc in each sc around, join with sl st in first sc (12 sc).

Round 3: Ch 1, (sc in next sc, 2 sc in next sc) 6 times; join with sl st in first sc (18 sc).

Round 4: Ch 1, (sc in each of next 2 sc, 2 sc in next sc) 6 times; join with sl st in first sc (24 sc).

Round 5: Ch 1, (sc in each of next 3 sc, 2 sc in next sc) 6 times; join with sl st in first sc (30 sc).

Round 6: Ch 1, (sc in each of next 4 sc, 2 sc in next sc) 6 times; join with sl st in first sc (36 sc).

Round 7: Ch 1, (sc in each of next 5 sc, 2 sc in next sc) 6 times; join with sl st in first sc (42 sc).

Round 8: Ch 1, (sc in each of next 6 sc, 2 sc in next sc) 6 times; join with sl st in first sc (48 sc).

Round 9: Ch 1, (sc in each of next 7 sc, 2 sc in next sc) 6 times; join with sl st in first sc (54 sc). Fasten off A.

Final Round: Draw up a loop of B in first sc of previous round, ch 1, *3 dc in next sc, sk next sc, sc in next sc; repeat from * around; join with sl st in first sc (eighteen 3-dc groups) **(figs. F and G)**.

Fasten off. With tapestry needle, weave in all ends.

waves doorstop

You know that door that keeps closing on you? Prop it open with this doorstop, made with a brick, three waves of color, and a flower in bloom.

Finished Measurements

- 8 x 4 x 2½ inches
  (20.3 x 10.2 x 6.4cm)

What You'll Need

- Basic Crochet Tool Kit, page 7

- Stitch. Rock. Love. Sheep(ish) (70% acrylic/30% wool; 3oz/85g = 167yds/153m): less than 1 ball each, (A) #0004 white(ish), (B) #0011 taupe(ish) (4)

- Stitch Nation Bamboo Ewe (55% viscose from bamboo/45% wool; 3.5oz/100g = 177yds/162m): less than 1 ball, (C) #5875 twilight (4)

- Rectangular brick: 8 x 4 x 2½ inches
  (20.3 x 10.2 x 6cm)
  Note: This doorstop was made with this brick size, but for variations, crochet to fit the brick on hand.

- Plastic ring, 1¹/₈ inches (2.9cm)

- Crochet hook: US E-4 (3.5mm) or size needed to obtain gauge

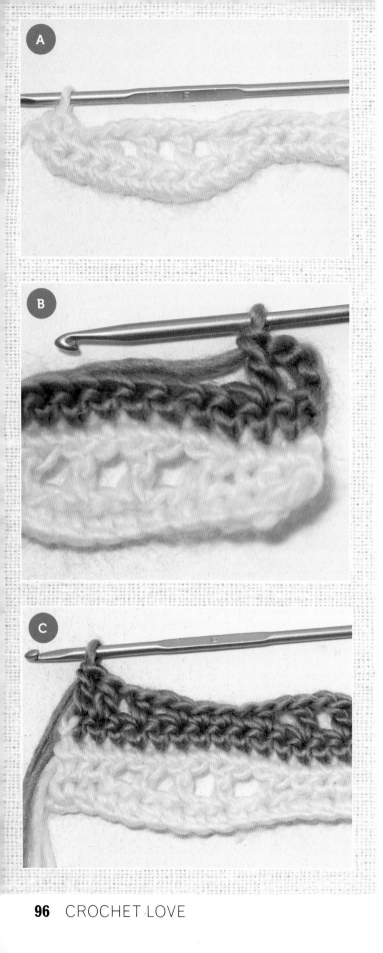

Gauge: Approximately 13 sts and 14 rows over 4 inches (10.2cm) of wavy pattern

Always take time to check the gauge or the finished measurement of the project as provided.

Abbreviations: See page 11.

Note: To change color, work last stitch of old color to last yarn over. Yarn over with new color and draw through all loops on hook to complete stitch. Proceed with new color. Fasten off old color.

Instructions

Wavy Rectangle

To begin: With A, ch 26.

Row 1: Sc in 2nd ch from hook, sc in each ch across, turn (you now have 25 sc).

Row 2: Ch 1, sc in next 2 sc, *ch 1, sk next sc, hdc in next sc, (ch 1, sk next sc, dc in next sc) 2 times, ch 1, sk next sc, hdc in next sc, ch 1, sk next sc, sc in next 3 sc; repeat from * once more, omitting the last sc, turn (10 ch-1 sps) **(fig. A)**.

Row 3: Ch 1, sc in each st and in each ch-1 sp across; change to B in last st, turn (25 sc).

Row 4: With B, ch 1, sc in each sc across, turn. Fasten off A.

Row 5: Ch 3 (counts as dc), dc in next sc, ch 1, sk next sc, hdc in next sc, ch 1, sk next sc, sc in next 3 sc, ch 1, sk next sc, hdc in next sc, (ch 1, sk next sc, dc in next sc) 2 times, ch 1, sk next sc; hdc in next sc, ch 1, sk next sc, sc in next 3 sc, ch 1, sk next sc, hdc in next sc, ch 1, sk next sc, dc in last 2 sc, turn (9 ch-1 sps) **(figs. B and C)**.

Row 6: Ch 1, sc in each st and ch-1 sp across, ending with sc in top of beginning ch-3; change to C in last st, turn (25 sc).

Row 7: With C, ch 1, sc in each sc across, turn. Fasten off B.

Repeat Rows 2–7, changing yarns every third row to repeatedly work 3 rows with A, 3 rows with B, and 3 rows with C **(fig. D)**, until piece is long enough to wrap around brick, stretching fabric slightly. Fasten off. With tapestry needle, weave in all ends.

Wrap the work around the brick and whipstitch the short ends together. Weave in all ends.

Brick Ends (Make 2) and Finishing

To begin: With C, ch 9.

Row 1: Sc in 2nd ch from hook and each ch across, turn (8 sc).

Rows 2–13: Ch 1, sc in each sc across, turn.

Fasten off, leaving a long tail for sewing piece to edges of wavy rectangle.

Place one of the end pieces against one end of the brick. Whipstitch the two pieces together along all four edges of the end piece. Repeat with second end piece. Weave in all ends.

Ring Ornament

Refer to the pattern for Ring #3 on page 117. Use A and B from this pattern to make the ring. Use A to stitch the ring to the brick.

freeform embellished skirt

Breathe new life into an old skirt with a touch of freeform crochet and a whisper of hand embroidery.

What You'll Need

- Basic Crochet Tool Kit, page 7
- Skirt
- Crochet Hemp, worsted weight hemp 12 (100% hemp; 1.1lb/500g = 425yds/392m): (A) less than 1 spool ④
- DMC Perle Cotton 5 (100% cotton; 5g = 27.3yds/25m): (B) less than 1 ball, 0310 black
- Crochet hook for A: US H-8 (5mm)
- Crochet hook for B: US B-1 (2.25mm)
- Taupe thread
- Sewing needle and thread

Abbreviations: See page 11.

Hemp Yarn Stalk #1

Hemp Yarn Stalk #2

Hemp Yarn Stalk #3

Black Perle Cotton Stalk #1

Black Perle Cotton Stalk #2

Stalk #1 made with crocheted chain stitch and embroidered seed stitches.

Instructions

Hemp Yarn Stalk #1

1 With A, create a chain of stitches that measures approximately 24 inches (61cm), or the length that is needed to work on your skirt. Do not fasten off until after you pin the work to the skirt, in case you need to adjust the length of the chain stitch.

2 Pin the crocheted chain to the skirt, beginning at the bottom edge and working upward. Create three "petals" along the way by twisting the crochet into loops and pinning them to the skirt. Make any adjustments by adding or removing chain stitches to finish the three petals and fasten off, leaving a long tail.

3 Sew the crochet chain to the skirt with needle and thread. Weave in all ends with a tapestry needle.

4 With B, embroider seed stitches in the centers of the petals.

Hemp Yarn Stalk #2

1 With A, create a chain of stitches that measures approximately 16 inches (40.6cm), or the length that is needed to work on your skirt. Do not fasten off until after you pin the work to the skirt, in case you need to adjust the length of the chain stitch.

2 Pin the crocheted chain to the skirt, beginning at the bottom edge and working upward. Create one petal at the very top of the stalk by twisting the crochet into a loop and pinning it to the skirt.

3 Sew the crochet chain to the skirt with needle and thread. Weave in all ends with a tapestry needle.

4 With B, embroider seed stitches in the center of the petal.

Hemp Yarn Stalk #3

1 With A, ch 3; join with a sl st in first ch to form a ring. Work 10 sc in the ring.

2 Fasten off, leaving a long tail. Pin the work to the skirt. Sew the circle portion to the skirt with hand sewing needle and thread. With sewing needle and B, embroider a running stitch around the circle portion and fasten the tails to the skirt with a couch stitch.

Black Perle Cotton Stalk #1

1 With B, ch 3; join with a sl st in first ch to form a ring. Work 10 sc in the ring.

2 Fasten off, leaving a long tail. Pin the work to the skirt. With sewing needle and B, sew the circle portion to the skirt, and fasten the tails to the skirt with a couch stitch.

Black Perle Cotton Stalk #2

1 With B, ch 1, work 5 sc in 2nd ch from the hook; join with a sl st in first sc (5 sc).

2 *Ch 1, (2 dc, ch 2, sl st) in next sc; repeat from * 4 more times to create 5 petals.

3 Fasten off, leaving a long tail. Pin the work to the skirt. With sewing needle and B, sew the flower portion to the skirt and fasten the tails to the skirt with a couch stitch.

Seed Stitch

Make small straight stitches of the same length in varying directions to fill in a shape with texture and color.

Couch Stitch

Lay yarn in one direction of the design. With another yarn, anchor it down at even intervals with a small stitch over the first yarn and into the fabric.

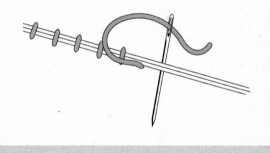

Running Stitch

Weave the needle through the fabric at evenly spaced intervals.

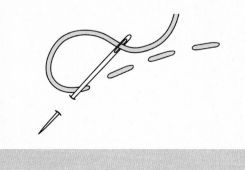

cocktail rings

Because these rings are crocheted with a combination of crochet thread and elastic thread, they have just the right amount of grip to stay put on your fingers—and just the right amount of "give" to be taken off easily.

Finished Measurements

- For Flower Ring: Flower: 1¾ inches (4.4cm) diameter, Band: ⅝ inch (1.6cm) wide
- For Heart Ring: Heart: ½ x ¾ inches (1.3 x 1.9cm), Band: ⅝ inch (1.6cm) wide

What You'll Need

- Basic Crochet Tool Kit, page 7

- Aunt Lydia's Bamboo Crochet Thread (100% viscose from bamboo; size 10; 300 yds/274m): less than 1 ball each, (A) #0275 coral and (B) #0320 mushroom (0)

- Gütermann elastic thread (64% polyester, 36% polyurethane; 11yds/10m): less than 1 spool each, (C) #5019 white and (D) #4017 black

- Crochet hook: US B-1 (2.25mm)

- Hand sewing needle

- Black thread

- Medium glass bead

- Small white button

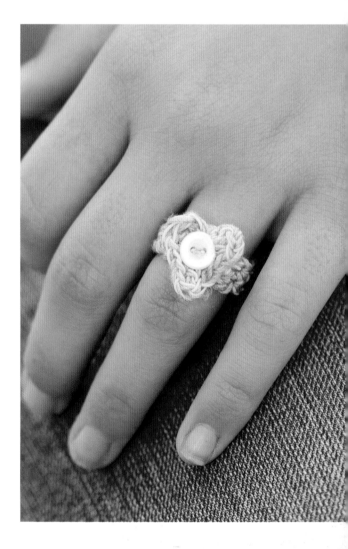

Gauge: Use finished measurements for gauge.

Always take time to check the gauge or the finished measurement of the project as provided.

Abbreviations: See page 11.

Instructions

Flower Ring Band

To begin: With one strand each of A and D held together, ch 4.

Row 1: Sc in 2nd ch from hook, sc in next 2 sc, turn (you now have 3 sc).

Row 2: Ch 1, sc in each sc across, turn.

Repeat Row 2 until piece is long enough to fit around your finger.

Fasten off. With a tapestry needle, whipstitch the two short ends together. The seam will be the center top of the band.

Flower

To begin: With one strand each of A and D held together, ch 2.

Round 1: Work 5 sc in 2nd ch from hook; join with sl st in first sc (5 sc).

Round 2: (Ch 5, sc in 2nd ch from hook, dc in each of next 2 ch, hdc in last ch **(fig. A)**, sl st in next sc of Round 1) 5 times, ch 5, sc in 2nd ch from hook, dc in next 2 ch, hdc in last ch, sl st in st at base of first petal to join (6 petals) **(fig B)**.

Fasten off. With tapestry needle, sew the flower to the center top of the band. With hand-sewing needle and black thread, sew the glass bead to the center of the flower.

Heart Ring Band

With one strand each of B and C held together, follow pattern for the Flower Ring Band to make a band.

Heart

With one strand each of B and C held together, ch 3, join with sl st in first ch to form a ring, ch 3, (2 dc, 3 sc) in ring, ch 1, dc in ring, ch 1, (3 sc, 2 dc) in ring, ch 2, sl st in ring **(figs. C and D)**.

Fasten off. With tapestry needle, sew the heart to the center top of the band. With hand sewing needle and B, sew a small white button to the center of the heart.

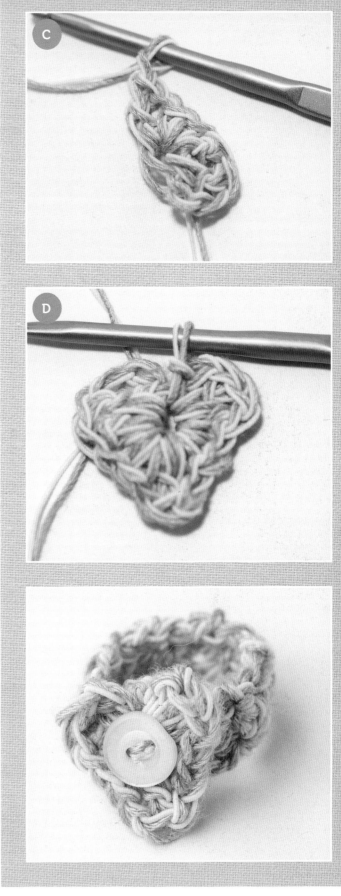

upcycled plastic tote

It's ever so sensible to save your plastic grocery bags, but how will you ever use them all? Here's an idea: Cut them up and make some plastic bag yarn (a.k.a. "plarn")—then crochet yourself a tote or two!

Finished Measurements

- Circumference: 21 inches (53.3cm)
- Height: 9 inches (22.9cm)
- Strap: 25 x 2½ inches (63.5 x 6.4cm)

What You'll Need

- Basic Crochet Tool Kit, page 7
- Plastic grocery bags, approximately 100 beige bags (A), and 10 white bags (B)
- Crochet Hook: US J-10 (6mm)

Gauge: Approximately 8 sts and 9 rows over 4 inches (10.2cm) of single crochet.

Always take time to check the gauge or the finished measurement of the project as provided.

Abbreviations: See page 11.

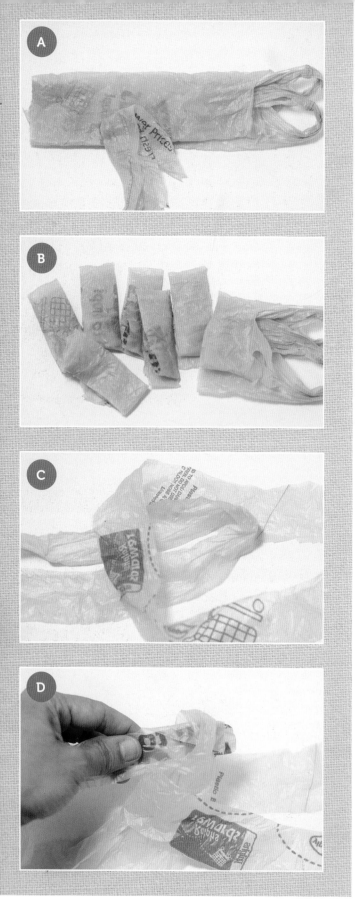

Instructions

Making the Plarn

1 Fold a grocery bag in half along its length, matching up the two top handles and the bottom corners. Fold the bag in half again two or three more times until the bag is folded into a thin strip.

2 Trim ½ inch (1.3cm) off the bottom edge and discard **(fig. A)**.

3 Cut across the folded bag about 1½ inches (3.8cm) up from the trimmed bottom edge. Cut more segments of the same width until you come to the bottom of the handles (you'll have 6 to 10 segments, depending on the size of the bag). Discard the excess handle portions of the bag **(fig. B)**.

4 Open the folded segments into large, open rings.

5 To join the ringed segments:
- Lay out two of the rings end-to-end, with the ends overlapping (with the second ring on top of the first ring) **(fig. C)**.
- Pick up the opposite end of the first ring and thread it into the loop between the two rings **(fig. D)**.
- Pull the inserted end until the loops are snugly joined **(fig. E)**.
- Repeat steps until all strips have become joined into one long strip, rolling the strip into a ball as you go.

Tote and Strap

To begin tote: With A, ch 4; join with sl st in first ch to form a ring.

Round 1: Ch 1, 6 sc in ring; join with sl st in first sc (you now have 6 sc) **(fig. F)**.

Round 2: Ch 1, 2 sc in each sc around; join with sl st in first sc (12 sc).

Round 3: Ch 1, (sc in next sc, 2 sc in nest sc) 6 times; join with sl st in first sc (18 sc).

Round 4: Ch 1, (sc in next 2 sc, 2 sc in next sc) 6 times; join with sl st in first sc (24 sc).

Round 5: Ch 1, (sc in next 3 sc, 2 sc in next sc) 6 times; join with sl st in first sc (30 sc).

Round 6: Ch 1, (sc in next 4 sc, 2 sc in next sc) 6 times; join with sl st in first sc (36 sc).

Round 7: Ch 1, (sc in next 5 sc, 2 sc in next sc) 6 times; join with sl st in first sc (42 sc).

Rounds 8–27: Ch 1, sc in each sc around; join with sl st in first sc.

To begin strap: Sc in next 5 sc, turn; leave remaining sts unworked (5 sc) **(fig. G)**.

Rows 1–45: Ch 1, sc in next 5 sc, turn **(fig. H)**.

Fasten off.

With tapestry needle, whipstitch the end of the strap to the top edge of the tote, so that it is aligned directly across from the beginning of the strap.

Fasten off.

With tapestry needle, weave in all ends.

Flower

Foundation Round: With B, ch 2, work 5 sc in 2nd ch from hook; join with sl st in first sc (5 sc).

Petals: *Ch 2, (dc, ch 2, sl st) in next sc; repeat from * 4 more times to create 5 petals.

Fasten off, leaving a long tail.

With tapestry needle, sew the flower to the top edge of the tote, centered in between the strap ends. Weave in all ends.

toddler crowns

Here's a project to enchant little tykes who like to imagine themselves as kings and queens.

Finished Measurements

- 15 inches (38.1cm) circumference

What You'll Need

- Basic Crochet Tool Kit, page 7

- Lion Brand Cotton-Ease (50% cotton/50% acrylic; 3.5oz/100g = 207yds/188m): less than 1 ball each, (A) #123 seaspray, (B) #134 terracotta (4)

- Aunt Lydia's Bamboo Crochet Thread (100% viscose from bamboo; size 10; 300yds/274m); less than 1 ball, (C) #226 natural (0)

- 10 yds (9m) black craft wire (D), 28-gauge

- Crochet hook: US E-4 (3.5mm)

Gauge: Approximately 12 sts and 13 rows over 4 inches (10.2cm) of single crochet worked with 1 strand each of A and D held together.

Always take time to check the gauge or the finished measurement of the project as provided.

Abbreviations: See page 11.

Instructions

Crown Base

To begin: With 1 strand each of A and D held together, ch 4, sc in 2nd ch from hook, sc in each of next 2 ch, turn (you now have 3 sc).

Rows 1–48: Ch 1, sc in each sc, turn.

Fasten off. With tapestry needle, whipstitch the two short ends together, weave in all ends.

Crown Top

Attach to the base: With 1 strand each of B and D held together, draw up a loop anywhere on one edge of the crown's base (for top of crown), ch 1, sc evenly around entire edge, join with sl st in first sc.

Next row: *Ch 6, sk next sc, sl st in next sc, sc in next sc; repeat from * around; join with sl st in base of beginning ch-6 (16 ch-6 spaces). Fasten off.

Crown top: Fold C to make a double strand that is approximately 12 inches (30.5cm) long and draw up a loop in one of the ch-6 spaces, ch 1, (yo, insert hook in same ch-6 space, yo and draw up a loop) 3 times, yo and draw yarn through all 7 loops on hook (puff made). Fasten off **(figs. A, B, and C)**.

Repeat for all ch-6 spaces.

With tapestry needle, weave in all ends.

Variation

Start with B for the Crown Base and finish with A for the Crown Top. Pinch the top centers of the scallops to make a pointy Crown Top. Fasten off. With tapestry needle, weave in all ends.

hanging rings

Keep things simple by making a hanging ring to adorn a gift or a doorknob—or make several in different colors to decorate a window or doorway.

Finished Measurements

- Ring #1: 1¼ inches (3.2cm) in diameter
- Ring #2: 1½ inches (3.8cm) in diameter
- Ring #3: 2 inches (5.1cm) in diameter
- Ring #4: 2½ inches (6.4cm) in diameter

Ring #3

Ring #2

Ring #1

Ring #4

What You'll Need

- Basic Crochet Tool Kit, page 7
- Patons Grace Mercerized cotton (100% mercerized cotton; 1.75oz/50g = 136yds/125m): less than 1 ball each, (A) #62044 clay; (B) #62322 viola (3)
- Aunt Lydia's Bamboo Crochet Thread (100% viscose from bamboo; size 10; 300 yds/274m): less than 1 ball each, (C) #226 natural; (D) #275 coral (0)
- Crochet hook: US C-2 (2.75mm)
- Plastic rings (8), 1⅛ inches (2.9cm)

Gauge: Use finished measurements for gauge.

Always take time to check the gauge or the finished measurement of the project as provided.

Abbreviations: See page 11.

Stitch Guide: Special Stitches

Join double-strand to ring: Fold length of yarn in half to work with a double strand. Place the folded section into the center of a plastic ring from back to front. Place the hook into the fold, take the hook over the top of the ring, yo with the double strand and draw it through the fold. Continue to work with a double strand **(figs. A and B)**.

Work sc in ring: Insert hook in center of ring, yo and draw loop through ring to front, take hook over the top of the ring, yo and draw through both loops on hook **(figs. C, D, and E)**.

Work dc in ring: Yo, insert hook in center of ring, yo and draw loop through ring to front, take hook over the top of the ring, (yo and draw through 2 loops on hook) twice **(figs. F, G, and H)**.

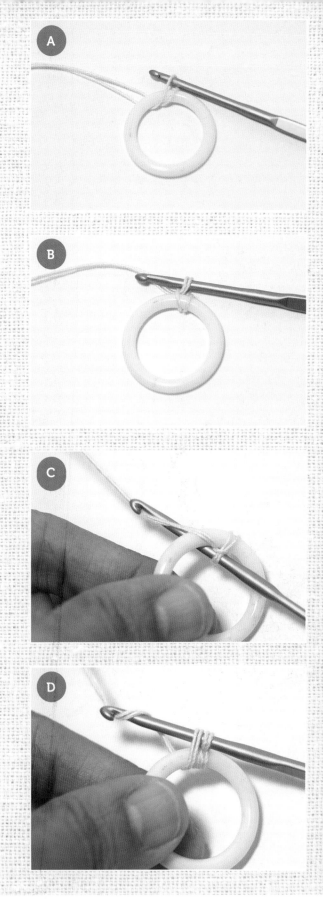

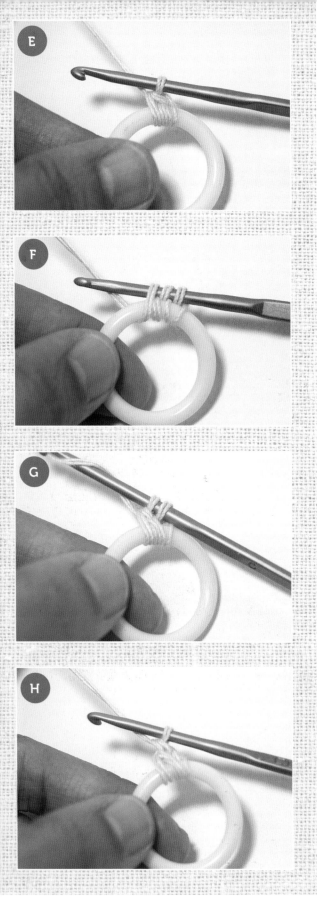

Instructions

Note: Make variations of all rings by using different combinations of yarns.

Ring #1

To begin: Pull out approximately 4 yards (3.7m) of C and join double-strand to ring.

Round 1: Ch 2, work 28 sc in ring; join with sl st in first sc.

Chain: Ch 30. Fasten off. With tapestry needle, weave in all ends **(fig. I)**.

Ring #2

To begin: Make Ring #1 with A.

Round 2: Draw up a loop of D in any sc of Round 1, ch 1, sc in each sc around; join with a sl st in first sc **(fig. J)**.

Round 3: *Ch 5, sk next sc, sl st in next sc; repeat from * around. Fasten off. With tapestry needle, weave in all ends **(fig. K)**.

Ring #3

To begin: Pull out approximately 10 inches (25.4cm) of A and join double-strand to ring.

Round 1: Ch 3 (counts as first dc), work 31 dc in ring; join sl st in top of beginning ch (32 dc).

Chain: Ch 30. Fasten off A.

Petals: Draw up a loop of B in any dc of Round 1, ch 3, sl st in 3rd ch from hook (picot made), sl st in next dc, *sc in next dc, picot, sl st in next dc; repeat from * around **(fig. L)**.

Fasten off.

With tapestry needle, weave in all ends.

Ring #4

To begin: Pull out approximately 10 inches (25.4cm) of B and join double-strand to ring.

Round 1: Ch 3 (counts as dc), work 31 dc in ring; join with sl st in top of beginning ch (32 dc).

Chain: Ch 30. Fasten off B.

Petals: Draw up a loop of yarn C in any dc of Round 1, ch 2, (2 dc and sl st) in same dc, sk next dc, *(3 dc and sl st) in next dc, sk next dc; repeat from * around; join with sl st in top of beginning ch **(fig. M)**.

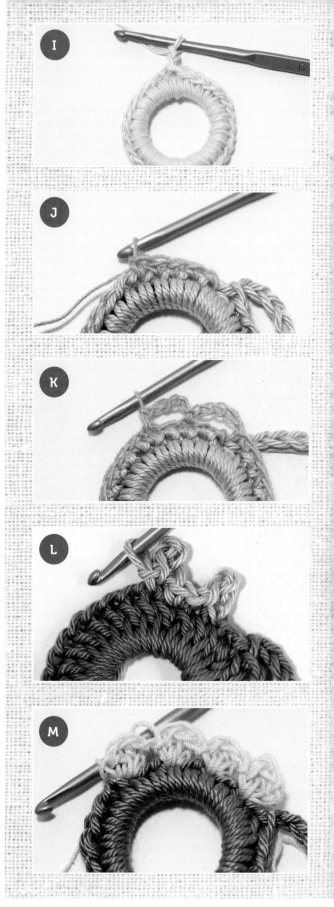

missoni-inspired necklace

Whip up this petite shimmery chevron-shaped necklace to add a little sparkle to your life.

Finished Measurements

- Crocheted chevron: 2 x 1 inches (5.1 x 2.5cm)

What You'll Need

- Basic Crochet Tool Kit, page 7
- Aunt Lydia's Bamboo Crochet Thread (100% bamboo; size 10; 300yds/274m): (A) less than 1 ball, #0320 mushroom (0)
- Loops & Threads Metallic Perle (22oz/6.5g): less than 1 ball each, (B) hot pink; (C) silver; (D) light pink
- Crochet hook: US C-2 (2.75mm)
- Small freshwater pearl
- Silver 28-gauge craft wire: 18 inches (45.7cm)
- 2-part silver chain necklace: 18 inches (45.7cm)
- Three silver jump rings
- Needle-nose pliers

Gauge: Use finished measurements for gauge.

Always take time to check the gauge or the finished measurement of the project as provided.

Abbreviations: See page 11.

Instructions

Shimmery Chevron

To begin: With one strand each of A and B held together, ch 12 + ch 2 (counts as first sc in Row 1).

Row 1: Sc in 3rd ch from hook and in next 3 ch, (sc2tog) 2 times, sc in next 3 ch, 2 sc in next sc, turn (you now have 12 sc, including the + ch 2 from the beginning that counts as 1 sc) **(fig. A)**.

Cut B, continue with one strand each of C and A held together.

Row 2: Ch 2 (counts as sc), sc in first 4 sc, (sc2tog) 2 times, sc in next 3 sc, 2 sc in next sc (the beginning ch-2), turn **(fig. B).**

Row 3: Repeat Row 2.

Cut C, continue with one strand each of D and A held together.

Rows 4 and 5: Repeat Row 2 twice.

Fasten off. Weave in ends with a yarn needle **(fig. C)**.

Yarn Bead Dangle and Chain

1 Thread the pearl with craft wire, and wrap pearl with wire repeatedly in many directions so that it looks like a ball of yarn. Trim excess wire **(fig. D)**.

2 Attach the pearl dangle to a jump ring using needle-nose pliers **(fig. E)**.

3 Attach the jump ring to the crocheted work.

4 Attach 2-part silver chain necklace to jump rings using needle-nose pliers.

5 Attach one jump ring with chain section to each top corner of the crocheted piece **(fig. F)**.

mason jar cozies

These cozies will make your mason jars look so inviting, you'll want to work up several to store all of your small treasures.

Finished Measurements

- Each cozy: 11¼ inches (28.6cm) in circumference x 3½ inches (8.9cm) in height

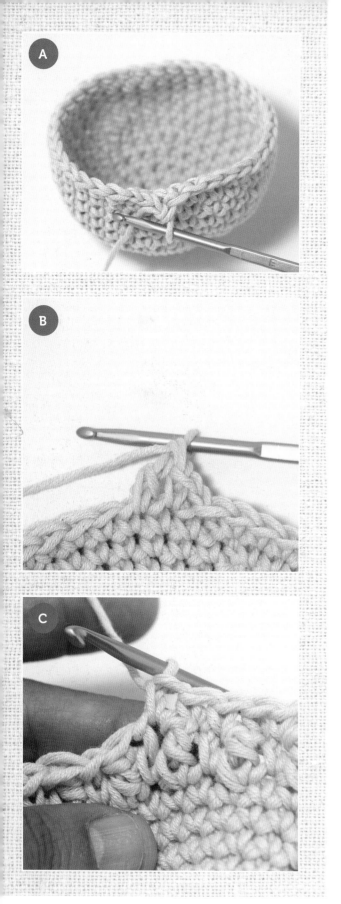

What You'll Need

- Basic Crochet Tool Kit, page 7
- Lion Brand LB Collection Cotton Bamboo (52% cotton/48% rayon; 3.5oz/100g = 245yds/224m): (A) less than 1 ball, #098 magnolia **(3)**
- Lily Sugar 'n Cream (100% cotton; 2.5oz/70g = 120yds/109m): (B) less than 1 ball, #00001 white **(4)**
- Crochet hook: US E-4 (3.5mm)
- 2 Mason jars, 10-ounce size

Gauge: Approximately 13 sts and 16 rows over 4 inches (10.2cm) of single crochet.

Always take time to check the gauge or the finished measurement of the project as provided.

Abbreviations: See page 11.

Instructions

Tan Cozy with White Trim

To begin: With A, ch 4; join with sl st in first ch to form a ring.

Round 1: Ch 1, 6 sc in ring; join with sl st in first sc (you now have 6 sc).

Round 2: Ch 1, 2 sc in each sc around; join with sl st in first sc (12 sc).

Round 3: Ch 1, (sc in next sc, 2 sc in next sc) 6 times; join with sl st in first sc (18 sc).

Round 4: Ch 1, (sc in next 2 sc, 2 sc in next sc) 6 times, join with sl st in first sc (24 sc).

Round 5: Ch 1, (sc in next 3 sc, 2 sc in next sc) 6 times, join with sl st in first sc (30 sc).

Round 6: Ch 1, (sc in next 4 sc, 2 sc in next sc) 6 times; join with sl st in first sc (36 sc).

Rounds 7–11: Ch 1, sc in each sc around; join with sl st in first sc **(fig. A)**.

Round 12: Ch 1, (sc in next sc, tr in next sc) 18 times; join with sl st in first sc **(fig. B)**.

Round 13: Ch 1, sc in each st around; join with sl st in first sc **(fig. C)**.

Rounds 14–17: Repeat last 2 rounds 2 times.

Rounds 18–22: Ch 1, sc in each sc around; join with sl st in first sc. Fasten off A.

Round 23: Draw up a loop of B in any sc, ch 1, (sc in next sc, tr in next sc) 18 times, join with sl st in first sc **(fig. D)**.

Fasten off. With tapestry needle, weave in all ends.

White Cozy with Tan Trim

To begin: With B, ch 4; join with sl st in first ch to form a ring.

Round 1: Ch 1, 6 sc in ring; join with sl st in first sc (you now have 6 sc).

Round 2: Ch 1, 2 sc in each sc around; join with sl st in first sc (12 sc).

Round 3: Ch 1, (sc in next sc, 2 sc in next sc) 6 times; join with sl st in first sc (18 sc).

Round 4: Ch 1, (sc in next 2 sc, 2 sc in next sc) 6 times, join with sl st in first sc (24 sc).

Round 5: Ch 1, (sc in next 3 sc, 2 sc in next sc) 6 times; join with sl st in first sc (30 sc).

Rounds 6–16: Ch 1, sc in each sc around; join with sl st in first sc. Fasten off B.

Round 17: Draw up a loop of A in any sc, ch 1, (sc in next sc, tr in next sc) 15 times, join with sl st in first sc **(fig. E)**.

Fasten off. With tapestry needle, weave in all ends.

resources

Suppliers

Yarn and crochet supplies are widely available on the Internet. These are just a few of the websites that will serve you well.

A.C. Moore Arts and Crafts
Crochet is just one of many crafts represented; you'll find books, yarns, threads, and hooks.
1-888-ACMOORE
www.acmoore.com

Bernat Yarn
Sells both yarn and crochet thread.
1-800-351-8356
www.bernat.com

Caron Yarns
Wide selection of yarns of all types.
www.caron.com

Coats & Clark
Needlecraft supplies; carries Aunt Lydia's crochet threads.
1-800-648-1479
www.coatsandclark.com

Crochet Hemp
Premium hemp yarn.
www.crochethemp.com

JoAnn Fabric and Crafts
Supplies for sewing, crochet, knitting, and crafts.
1-888-739-4120
www.joann.com

Herrschners
Craft supplier for knitting, crochet, needlework, and beading.
www.herrschners.com
1-800-411-0838

Knit One Crochet Two
Yarn, patterns, and kits for yarn and crochet.
1-207-892-9625
www.knitonecrochettoo.com

KnitPicks
Sells crochet hooks, knitting needles, yarns, patterns; numerous online tutorials, including some videos.
1-800-574-1323
www.knitpicks.com

Lily Sugar 'n Cream
Specializes in yarns made from natural fibers.
1-800-351-8356
www.sugarncream.com

Lion Brand Yarn
Wide selection of yarns of all types.
www.lionbrand.com

Michaels
Well-known craft supplier, primary source of Loops & Threads yarn.
1-800-642-4235
www.michaels.com

Patons
Yarns (including mercerized cotton), patterns, and pattern books.
1-800-351-8357
www.patonsyarns.com

Red Rock Threads
Sells a wide range of Gütermann threads.
775-751-9972
www.guttermanthread.com

Roberts Arts & Crafts
Large selection of threads (including elastic thread) and sewing supplies.
www.robertscrafts.com

Stitch Nation
Sells superwash, Peruvian wool, bamboo, and alpaca yarns; many free patterns for both knitting and crochet.
www.stitchnationyarn.com

Thread Art
Good source for perle cotton and other embroidery threads.
1-800-504-6867
www.threadart.com

The Twinery
Specializes in Baker's Twine in an array of colors.
www.thetwinery.com

Vickie Howell Sheep(ish) Yarn
1-800-351-8356
www.bernat.com/vickiehowell

Webs
Huge selections of yarn (including hemp) for knitting and crochet; good sales.
1-800-367-9327
www.yarn.com

Websites for Learning More about Crochet

www.crochet.org
The official website of the Crochet Guild of America; you'll find plenty of how-to information here.

www.craftyarncouncil.com
This Craft Yarn Council website covers the basics and includes illustrated directions for crochet stitches.

crochet.about.com
Online videos walk you through basic crochet procedures.

www.stitchguide.com
Here's another source with illustrated instructions for crochet stitches.

editor: amanda carestio
art director: shannon yokeley
graphic designer: raquel joya
photographers: cynthia shaffer, jenny doh
cover designer: raquel joya
technical editor: kj hay
copyeditors: nancy d. wood, amanda crabtree weston
assistant editors: kerri winterstein, monica mouet
models: jenny doh, sierra reynolds, kara cailse

index

A
Apple Cozy Sling 20

B
Baby's Egg Rattle 44
Basics 7
Bear Ears Headband 48
Binder Duvet 24
Birthday Cake Bunting
    + Cupcake Picks 27
Bunting with Hearts 86

C
Camera Strap Cover
    + Lens Cap Pouch 56
Cocktail Rings 102

E
Embellished Knee-Highs . . . 60

F
Finger Puppets 78
Four-Fish Mobile 74
Freeform Embellished Skirt . . 98

G
Granny Square Belt 36

H
Hanging Rings 113
Heart Purse 30

L
Lemonade Coasters
    + Glass Cozies 70

M
Mason Jar Cozies 122
Missoni-Inspired Necklace . .118

P
Pretty Paperweights 52

S
Skinny Scalloped Scarf 63
Soap Saver + Washcloth 66

T
Table of Contents 5
This Little House 83
Tic Tac Toe 41
Toddler Crowns 110

U
Upcycled Chair Cushion . . . 90
Upcycled Plastic Tote 106

W
Waves Doorstop 94
Welcome 6

acknowledgments + dedication

I thank Kj Hay for providing unparalleled expertise and patience as the technical editor for this book. I thank Nancy D. Wood for her thorough copyediting work throughout the process. I thank Amanda Carestio for her collaborative spirit and professionalism. I thank the rest of my team members who made it all come together with quality and efficiency: Raquel Joya, Cynthia Shaffer, Amanda Crabtree Weston, Kerri Winterstein, and Monica Mouet.

I dedicate this book to all who share my passion for a minimalist design aesthetic as we demonstrate to the world the art and beauty of less.

about the author

Jenny Doh is head of *www.crescendoh.com*. She has authored and packaged numerous books including *Craft-a-Doodle*, *Print Collective*, *Creative Lettering*, *Stamp It!*, *Journal It!*, *We Make Dolls!*, *Hand in Hand*, and *Signature Styles*. She lives in Santa Ana, California, and loves to create, stay fit, and play music.